For

MW01253851

Crown HER a King ™

Restoring God's Glory to the Bride of Christ

Book One:

Cancerous Chaldee ™

Susan Dewbrew

Cover design by Renee Story
storyofrenee@gmail.com

Edited by Robert Savage
rom61314@ymail.com

BurkhartBooks
www.burkhartbooks.com
Bedford, Texas

Endorsements

The primary purpose of this book is to take the Church from the glory that She presently expresses to a coming greater glory. This book was written to allow the Church to develop into Her fullness. We are to be the manifest sons of God, which simply means that we are to be in a progressive state of constant maturing, and that our purpose as the Bride of Christ is to reproduce sons and daughters who will do greater works than the prior generations.

Susan Dewbrew's book is a book not only for the Church of now, but also for the Church of tomorrow. Despite our prior misunderstanding of 1 Corinthians 14:34 (which says, "women are to keep silent in the church for they are not permitted to speak"), I believe with all my heart that God is speaking prophetically and releasing revelation through His women. Women are called to prophesy, preach, teach, and lay hands on the sick. They are called to come down from the mountaintop. The mountain will open; the wings upon it will open up, and the women will come down as in chariots. "The Lord gives the word [of power]; the women who bear and publish [the news] are a great host (Psalm 68:11, AMP)." *Crown Her a King* will indeed raise up a greater company of women for the end-time glory of the Church.

JOHN P. KELLY
Convening Apostle,
International Coalition of Apostles
Fort Worth, Texas

My dad was the greatest Christian I have ever known, a man's man. A man not given to show much emotion. And yet when I was just a boy I saw my father break down and cry... and it was at the preaching of one of God's most anointed vessels—a woman!

This book, filled with truth, wisdom and revelation from God's Word will destroy the myth and lie that women have no place in the church. Every pastor who struggles with this issue should prayerfully read *Crown Her a King*. I encourage the body of Christ to read this word God has given Susan Dewbrew so that you will be set free by the truth!

BISHOP GARY OLIVER
Senior Pastor, Tabernacle of Praise
Singer, Songwriter, Speaker, TBN Host
Benbrook, Texas

Susan Dewbrew is a force to be reckoned with. We worked side by side for five years at Convergence Church in Fort Worth, Texas, and I watched as she poured her heart and life into the body of Christ. She created systems for ministries that are still operational today. She is a builder. Her heart is as big as the state of Texas. It is no surprise that our Heavenly Father would ask her to tackle a worldwide issue. That is the issue of redeemed women standing together with redeemed men in their callings before God, in His kingdom, and in the local church.

RICK MONTGOMERY
Associate Pastor, Convergence Church
Fort Worth, TX

Susan and I worked closely together in church administration for years. That is where I discovered how the Lord gifted her with magnificent teaching skills, both one-on-one and to large groups. She possesses a God-given ability to bring truth and equip in an extremely positive and encouraging way, whether on how to do a mail merge, or find the Greek root of a word in Scripture! I love that about my friend Susan!

Crown Her a King is a message totally rooted and grounded upon the Gospel of Grace: The Gospel of the Kingdom. Susan has bravely gone where very few have dared to go on "the woman issue," discovering error that must be reconciled with His Truth. I have listened to many expound on this issue, but NEVER have I EVER had anyone submit evidence that demands a verdict and confirms research that undeniably aligns with God's Truth on the matter! This has been a missing and necessary element to bring understanding about God's brilliant and effective plan for man and woman to subdue the earth together as one! Susan's heart beats with the Father's passion for His Bride. In the pages of this series, Susan uncovers both God's original intent and blueprint to ultimately and fully restore His Bride's glory. It is a message that WILL change the world!

JEANIE KUNERTH
Shining sWord Ministries
El Cajon de Grecia, Costa Rica

As a former student of mine, Susan excelled in her course assignments and even went beyond the requirements and did her own extensive research on the subject of women. She has continued her study, and in *Crown Her a King* she has passionately taken ownership of the vision of being a world changer where God's plan for woman is concerned. Her conversational way of writing makes for easy reading as she brings out the fallacy of the traditional teaching on women, which she supports with solid Biblical proof. She has a very interesting "take" on the Kingdom of God as it relates to the role of women. I encourage every man and woman to read this series of books, laying down your preconceived ideas regarding women and giving the Holy Spirit a chance to speak truth to your heart.

JOANNE KRUPP
Author, *WOMAN: God's Plan not Man's Tradition*
Professor, Christian Leadership University
Salem, Oregon

I remember meeting Susan for the first time in a class that we hold for new members at Convergence Church. It did not take me long to realize that she was not a "normal" church member. Susan jumped in right away. First, helping out as a volunteer and then coming on staff full time in the area of administration. We sat in my office and talked and prayed many times over the years as she faced days of discouragement, disappointment, and betrayal with honesty, transparency, and a courage to face her own weaknesses.

I watched as love found her again, and with that came a new direction in ministry, family additions, physical healing, and fresh vision. The one thing that never changed in all those years was Susan's passion for women stepping into all that God had created them to fulfill, including ministry. Again, I can remember standing in her study as she talked about her research and revelation concerning the role of women in the church—not from a place of bitterness or anger over how women have been mistreated over the years, but rather, from a heart excited about what God has for His bride in this new day.

I believe that she has a huge role in revealing His heart for women in this season.

TOM DERMOTT
Overseer, Transformations & Family Ministries
Convergence Church
Fort Worth, Texas

It has been our privilege to walk with Susan for a number of years and to see the integrity, gifting, and love for God that she carries. She is a powerful strategist and teacher. Her desire for all to know their value and identity as children of a beautiful, loving, powerful Father is inspiring and empowering.

We look forward to reading these books and exploring how we can see women and men fully activated and taking their places of honor and gifting in the body of Christ.

STEVE & MARCI FISH
Senior Leaders, Convergence Church
Fort Worth, Texas

Dedication

I dedicate this book to my amazing husband, Gregory L. Dewbrew.

Gregory, your life is the clearest demonstration I have ever seen of what Jesus looks like with skin on. You made your life an offering for those less fortunate than you, and you give up so much in order to feed the poor every day. You stood firm through two decades of celibacy because loyalty and marriage were a higher value to you than your own needs or desires. Then just a few years ago you took me as your wife, and I have watched you daily put our newly blended family before yourself—even to the point of spending your mornings with God on a hard closet floor.

Without your strength and determination *Crown Her a King* would not have survived the ferocious battle it has taken to get this far. The enemy has been relentless, waging every kind of warfare possible to prevent this message from reaching the Body of Christ. So many times I was afraid and ready to quit, but you stood firm. In this short time we have not only suffered ministry disappointments, but our new family has endured major financial loss, serious health issues, children and grandchildren moving in with us, a home robbery while we slept, and a major auto accident. That does not even begin to mention the constant pressure from those who still want to control and manipulate the Bride.

Thankfully, it has not just been the worst of times it has also been the very best of times. We have celebrated the birth of three wonderful grandchildren. And for me personally, you make my life complete. You are an amazing husband and friend. I am so blessed that you love me. And despite all the trials,

God has done incredible things. Many lives have been powerfully changed. Multitudes have grown in their knowledge of God's Kingdom on earth, and most importantly they have grown in their understanding of who they are in Christ. The chains binding them to darkness are being loosed as the light of truth dawns; they are to reign as kings on this earth but in a very different Kingdom. Your prophetic gifting and persistent servanthood made it happen. So many people have been set free from lies that kept them locked in the devil's dungeon; now they are ready to step out and fulfill their destiny!

Gregory, because you are a man after God's own heart, you have been willing to stand up and defend truth even at great cost. You have been willing to stand up for women in the church—and ultimately for the entire Bride of Christ. Thank you for being a genuine warrior coming to our rescue. Thank you for being strong enough to lift me up. Thank you for keeping me by your side even when it would have been much easier to just step in front and take over.

Thank you for demonstrating what a king in the Kingdom on earth truly looks like. I love you, and I know that together with Christ we are going to change the world!

Acknowledgements

Thanks to Debbie Cole for carrying me, my family, and this entire project in prayer through the past few years. At times it felt like we were giving birth to an elephant. There were moments I thought it was not worth the delay or the agony—but you pressed in, so we all pressed on. May you share in all the spoils of victory!

Thanks also to Linda Shebesta and Claudette McGuffee for linking arms with Debbie during the production of Book One; you formed a prayer shield around me that was truly the difference between life and death. Also to Bob Savage who has consistently and faithfully carried our family, ministries, and children in prayer. Thank you all for your sacrifice; joining forces made us strong. You are living proof that prayer makes a difference!

There are also so many prayer warriors who faithfully and regularly carry us and this message before the Throne. We would not be here if it were not for you!! We are one huge team!!!

Levi Davis, you are a man of the new generation in God's Army. Your radical obedience and generous giving made *Crown Her a King* possible. Without you I could not have finished the race. And I sincerely believe that it was a prophetic act demonstrating it will be today's young men of valor who will defeat the enemy and rescue the Bride. Thank you for being a true warrior!

Jeanie Kunerth, for transcribing the audio teaching of *"Cancerous Chaldee."* It was a labor of love, and I am so grateful for the many hours you poured into this project. I've watched you pour your life and talent into the Kingdom on a voluntary, full time basis for years. May the Lord bring you and Mark such quality laborers as you move onto the international scene. Thank you both for your consistent giving. You truly live the life of Grace that you preach.

Lisa Kay Fletcher, for help with the title, editing, continually encouraging me, and for standing with me when it made no sense in the natural. Thank you for being a true friend.

Angela Stephens, for believing in me and for re-purposing my wardrobe (laughing out loud—fashion is not my gift). Thanks, my friend, for helping us press forward into all God has in store.

Renee Story, for using her creative gifts to express the message in my heart into the cover art of *Crown Her a King*, as well as for all the marketing help with Kingdom Brewing and Dewbrew Realty. We so appreciate you pouring into us.

Gary Galloway, for being like a spiritual father to me and for consistently and repeatedly telling me to write. Look, Gary, I did it! :-)

And to all those who unselfishly demonstrated the Kingdom message by praying or serving during the live class, thank you! There are too many of you to name here, but because you all served in such a humble and Christ-like manner, many lives are still being blessed! ***Love wins!***

Books in the Series

Book One: *Cancerous Chaldee*

Book Two: *The Gospel of the Kingdom*

Book Three: *Who's the Helper?*

Book Four: *Lies that Bind*

Book Five: *The Groom's Voice*

Book Six: *Your Royal Identity*

Book Seven: *Taking Dominion*

Book Eight: *Nobility's Rule*

Book Nine: *United We Stand…*

Book Ten: *True Worship, True Love*

Book Eleven: *The Great Mystery*

Book Twelve: *Her Coronation*

See **About the Series** at the end of this book
for a short synopsis of each of these power-packed books!

Contents

Foreword

I love this book! I love the title. I love the spirit of it. And I love the revelation truths it has for all of us. Thank you, Susan, for your faithful obedience to both the Word and the Spirit which has produced this incredible gift to the Body of Christ.

In what many would find a daunting task, Susan invites us to re-visit some of the most controversial and misunderstood Scriptures in our Bibles.

Ten years ago the Lord began to take Susan on a journey revealing His heart for His Bride. Our paths intersected when she enrolled in distance learning classes with our online school, Christian Leadership University. As a graduate student, Susan excelled in her work, and we posted two of her final course papers on our website to be a blessing and resource to others. It is thrilling to see how the Lord used her studies with Christian Leadership University as a stepping-stone on her journey. We are excited and grateful to God to see the incredible fruit and ministry being born through her life!

With refreshing optimism and not a hint of the feminist Jezebel spirit, Susan invites us to travel with her as she discovers more of God's plan for women, His Church and indeed, the world. In what could potentially be a divisive presentation, Susan's sweet spirit and sincere humility make her message easy to receive, as does her passionate love for Christ and His Church which come shining through on every page.

And please note: this is not simply a book about the "women's issues". As important as they are, there is more here than that. The Lord has given Susan a two-fold revelation which also includes key insights on what it means to be a "king and priest" ruling and reigning with Christ. Her perspective on Kingdom living, what that looks like, and how we should every day be bringing heaven to earth, is equally powerful. I wholeheartedly agree with this message. The Kingdom of heaven is not a far off place. As we release Christ and His life and power out through our lives in supernatural ways, miracles manifest and it is done here on earth as it is in heaven!

I believe because Susan's heart was in the right place—not seeking to just prove what she wanted to believe—but really wanting to know and understand God's heart on this subject she came to truth. Indeed, the Spirit of Truth Himself opened wide His Scriptures, took the blinders off and revealed the very mind of Christ to Susan on this matter in a powerful way.

First, God spoke with a *rhema* word to Susan's heart. Next, He shared another glimpse of His message through a dream given to her in the night. So God supernaturally imparted His revelation knowledge to her listening heart. I love how this teaching was birthed out of the voice and vision of God! His supernatural handprints are all over it, while it is firmly grounded in Scripture, absolutely holding fast to the Word and clinging wholly to the divinely inspired soundness of it. She has dug deep into the Scriptures and brings us new insights from both the Old and New Testaments.

In this well-documented work, Susan is quick to point out how important it is not to jump from one error to another, taking an extreme position on the other side or harboring any bitterness or hurt against those who teach something different from this. The enemy is not each other (men and women), the enemy is satan. We should work together to subdue him, not try to put down and subdue one another. Susan states that "forgiveness is the toll to the road of freedom", and she is careful to never once let this pure message devolve into male bashing or any spirit of criticism or condemnation. Instead Susan rightfully declares, "Unity is the key to power, and honor is the key to unity."

Indeed, God has been emphasizing 1 Peter 2:17 to my heart over and over this past year: We are to "honor all people (NASB)." ALL people, all mankind, everyone—including women. Susan's teaching on honoring one another's differences (as man and woman) resonates with me, because the Lord has been teaching me this as well. To be sure, this message is timely for us all.

I can personally affirm that the revelations Susan shares in this book have proven true in my own life. My wife Patti has been my co-partner in ministry throughout our 40 years of marriage. From church planting and discipleship to writing and curriculum development, I could not have done it without her. I am the first to admit I would never have been as effective in ministry without Patti and the gifts and anointing God has placed within her. Together, we are a team—so much more together than either of us would be separately. That is how it is designed to be—corporately, together, in unity expressing the glory of God in the earth.

Susan explains from Genesis how this is in fact God's original intention! He is a Trinity, plurality in One. As humans created in His image, we are also a plurality, the two as one. That is where the fullness of His glory can be seen. As Susan says, "Man and wife were to be a plural unity, in God's image." The most complete representation and image of God on earth is God in man and woman together.

I think so often as leaders we recognize the amazing gifts and talents in our wives (and daughters and friends) and we know without a doubt that we are absolutely better because of them. Their anointings complete us and make us better and stronger! But then there seem to be certain verses in the Bible that somehow do relegate women to a different place than men. And we wonder, "How do we reconcile the two?" We see God in our wives! We see His anointing and wisdom and compassion in Christian women. Is there really a lesser anointing on them? Are they really not allowed to teach men, and must they "be silent" in the church as so many of us understand 1 Corinthians to teach?

As Susan writes, "Most church leaders today know that discrimination and lack of freedom are contrary to God's love, so they're confused and torn between Paul's words and God's heart." Thankfully, *Crown Her a King* is going to reconcile the discrepancies and free these leaders to follow God's heart and His Word!

I also appreciate the Discussion Questions and Private Time Questions in the Appendix section. The book is full of great revelation. But the only truth that changes us is what we actually apply to our lives. These thoughtful questions help us do just that and really make the principles our own by journaling with the Lord about the topic and hearing what He wants to speak personally to us about it.

Filled with hope, faith and contagious enthusiasm,

Susan inspires us to live in God's original design for both men and women—taking dominion together over the earth, bringing God's supernatural Kingdom to our everyday lives by ruling and reigning with Him.

Please read this important book with an open mind and most of all, an open heart. Let the Holy Spirit reveal all the Truth He has to share with you on this crucial subject. You will learn things you've never known before. You will come away with a fresh understanding of familiar Scriptures. You will find peace from the tension and questions you've had about women in ministry and leadership. You will be blessed!

MARK VIRKLER
President,
Christian Leadership University
Buffalo, New York

Mark is the author of over 50 books including *Dialogue with God* and *How to Hear God's Voice*.

One

Read Me First

*A strange title for the first chapter of a book? Maybe, but it worked. You are now reading the introduction. Too often intros are skipped because they are deemed as peripheral material, not important to the story. In this case, I want to take a moment to set the stage and briefly lay a foundation that will enable you to receive the full impact of the message in the **Crown Her a King** series. Thank you for starting at the beginning. It is my prayer that the transformative message of this book will change your world.*

Crown Her a King… when you read the title, did you squirm a bit? What do you think when you read statements like "women in authority" or "women in power". What images do such statements bring to your mind? How do they make you feel? Do you shudder from the thought of a woman in charge? Did the bottom of your stomach tighten up just a bit?

If so, was it because you have experienced Jezebel-like or over-controlling manipulating women? Or was it because the Bible teaches that women should not have authority over men and therefore should not be in power? Are you fearful of a book entitled "*Crown Her a King*?" Could it be because it sounds like "feminism" in the church? Does it sound like heresy or biblical error?

Even if it feels uncomfortable for a bit, hang in there! I invite you to take this journey with me… I promise it will be worth the trip. I promise what you learn will be biblically sound. Whether you are male or female, you will feel century old chains breaking off you! You will come to understand your true, royal identity and your dominion on the earth. You will be empowered to change your own world as well as to bring Kingdom influence to the world around you. Together, we will see the darkness in world systems diminish as the light of love and freedom reign through us.

The development of this material occurred through a decade long journey. It has been an interesting road, traveling the path of truth to personal freedom. The Lord could not reveal it all to me in a moment, because my heart as well as my head had to learn to think differently. Even though I knew the Bible well, His Kingdom was so very different that my thoughts did not line up with His thoughts. Therefore, we also will take this journey together one step at a time. *Cancerous Chaldee* is only the first of a series of 12 small, power-packed books on the subject of the believer's royal identity in Christ. Throughout the series, we are going to see where God honestly stands on the subject of women in the Kingdom, and we are going to see exactly how and why the Church at large got it so wrong! Because this book is biblically grounded, it will revolutionize the Church's teaching on women in ministry.

Regardless of your gender, it will also revolutionize your personal understanding of where you fit in God's Kingdom. You see, *Crown Her a King* is not just a book about women for women; it is about **Restoring God's Glory to the Bride of Christ**—the entire Body of Christ! Yes, it is about the "women in leadership" issue, but honestly there is much more to it than just that. **It is about Christ's Church, and it is about understanding God's Kingdom on the earth.** This book, and the whole series, is also for men who are in leadership and struggle with where women fit. As we come to grasp more fully the Kingdom of God, a veil is lifted from our understanding so we can readily see how and why we botched the women issue so badly. When I use the term "the women issue," I am referring to the issue of the female's gender being the deciding factor to determine her place or role in church and society.

Man's bride—the woman—represents Christ's Bride—the Church. When man's bride is restricted or held back, she is prevented from becoming all that she could possibly be. Her identity is diminished and her glory veiled. In the same fashion, when Christ's Bride is restricted or held back, She is prevented from becoming all that She could possibly be. Her identity is diminished and Her glory veiled.

Humans have had a long history of distorting God's will. Look around. God's plan is not this destructive, self-centered, godless society we live in. His will was both the beauty and intimacy of the Garden, as well as the adventure of battling the enemy and subduing the earth. Sadly, all of that got perverted. Instead of subduing the earth, we began to subdue each other. It was never God's plan that women be

25

restricted or held back in any manner. After millennia of misunderstanding God's intention toward women, He is on the move to restore her glory, for the hearts of men are now ready to receive the truth.

It is time for Christ's Bride, the Church, to become all God destined for Her to be—a glorious Bride, worthy of her Majestic Groom. You are part of that Bride! Come with me on this journey to freedom and discover the glory God created for you. It will not only change your life forever, it will change the world!

Two

Why Send Mary?

At age 35, I underwent a radical spiritual transformation. In my reasoning, that is when I truly became a Christ-follower. I was not raised in a traditional Christian home, but my mom raised me to believe in the basic tenants of the Christian faith. As a child, I said the sinner's prayer, I was baptized, and I definitely believed in Jesus. I did, but most of what I believed would have fit on a greeting card.

I believed my theology, but if I had to explain it, the whole thing would have sounded like a Hallmark Card—short and sweet. I believed Jesus was the Son of God; I believed He died for my sins; He was born on Christmas and raised on Easter. I genuinely believed, but that is all I knew. More importantly, I did not have a personal relationship with Christ. As I grew up, I matured in the world outside the church. I believed in Jesus, but it was the kingdoms of the world that influenced my thinking most.

Fast forward a few decades, now at 35 years of age with two wonderful kids, I began genuinely seeking the Lord. During this season of transformation, I faithfully attended church, devoured the Bible, and participated in every Bible study class I could find.

I soon ran into a real problem. In my world outside the church, women could become anything they aspired to be. The sky was the limit. Every person has an inalienable right to life, liberty, and the pursuit of happiness. No longer were these rights merely

> In my world outside the church, I had lots of experience with women in positions of power and authority.

given to aristocratic, white males. In my generation, we believe everybody has an opportunity to be a success, make their dreams come true, or be a world changer—everybody. You might have to overcome extreme challenges and hardships, but the field of life is open to all who are serious about the game.

After getting my bachelor's degree, I was on the fast track to success. I worked for a large corporation whose primary customers were the military and the airlines. It was both exciting and challenging. I worked hard and within a short period of time, I was promoted to management. My boss was a female and her boss was a female. There were plenty of men in leadership too; it was probably just coincidental that both my department and my division were led by women. I did not even know that when I chose the position. Prior to this job my former boss was also a female, an entrepreneur who built a software development company.

In my world outside the church, I had lots of experience with women in positions of power and authority. I had every intention of becoming one of them, for that was perfectly acceptable. It was not about "being somebody" or having recognition from other people. It was about having significance and value. I could make a difference and bring positive change to the world around me. In my personal experience, there was nothing negative about a woman operating in leadership.

In previous generations that was not always true. I saw only a few pockets of chauvinism in the workplace. The playing field was based on merit (at least in idealistic, modern thinking), e.g. productivity, creativity, leadership, loyalty—not on race, gender, or social status.

After giving birth to my first child, Benjamin, my heart wanted to stay home. I could not imagine anyone else raising him. But in the world's view, staying home was deemed less valuable than climbing the corporate ladder. The world did not esteem the role of a wife and mother. These competing systems caused an internal conflict. To have significance in the world, I had to be a successful leader, but my heart yearned to stay home with Ben. That is what I did. I followed my heart.

Two and half years later, I was doubly blessed as my daughter, Jaclyn, joined our family. I loved my children (still do!), and I was so incredibly grateful that I was financially able to stay home and be their main caregiver. Even though I found work I could do from home, it was just never the same. In giving up my career I felt like I had lost my identity and my ability to make a difference in the world. That is until I had this radical encounter with Christ and got plugged into a Bible-believing church.

You see, in my first church, being a stay-at-home

mom was highly esteemed. Once again, I felt valued for my daily service in life. I could actually make a difference in the world by pouring myself into my home. Family matters! It matters significantly, and thanks to this church, I was now able to put words to why my heart yearned to stay home. As a result of my choice to put family first, I experienced a level of freedom and value that I could not find in the world outside the church.

This is important for moms to understand. What you do is so important! Your service is valuable! Not just to your family, but to society at large and to God's Kingdom! You are shaping lives and building the next generation. If you do not have the ability to stay home, there is no condemnation! Single income families have it tough, especially in single parent homes. God will see you through this important season of your life, all you have to do is ask Him. He will help you protect and nurture your children. Never abdicate your role as primary caregiver, even if someone else is watching them while you work. You must raise your own children and be their godly role model. Be the number one influence in their life by staying connected heart to heart. You cannot tell them how to love and how to live— you must show them day in and day out. Your connection (or the lack thereof) with their heart will survive long past all the dinners, chores, school-

> Being a caregiver... is a vital, life-changing role.

ing, sports, and friends. Being a caregiver (whether you get to do it full-time or not) is a vital, life-changing role.

On the flip side, it did not take me long to discover that being a wife and mom was really all this church esteemed for women. It did not matter if a female was gifted or anointed, there were restrictions placed on her solely because of her gender. An altogether different internal conflict began to brew. God was now putting dreams and desires in my heart for ministry that made no sense in this environment. Being female, I could not be in leadership. I could not manage. I could not even teach (except other women or children). There was a clear division between the adult men and everyone else. A thick glass ceiling was blatantly present in the church that was not present in the work place.

It felt strange to gain freedom in some areas just to lose it in others.

That was a wonderful, fundamentalist-type church, superb at teaching the Bible. Many of the Sunday School classes were actually better than the classes I later took in seminary. They were deep and incredibly thorough. Most of all, they taught me to fully appreciate the Bible as the Word of God. I measure everything against it; the Bible is my plumb line. This is one thing I want you to be sure of

> It felt strange to gain freedom in some areas, just to lose it in others.

31

> If the Word says something is true, then I believe it...

as we begin this journey together. *Crown Her a King* may be revolutionary, but it is still biblically sound! There is nothing in this book that goes against the Word of God. If the Word says something is true, then I believe it, and that settles it.

Like so many other churches, that one believed the Bible taught that women must be under male leadership, and therefore females cannot be in authority nor can they teach adult men. That was their standard. At first, I believed what they said was true. As I began to study the Word of God, I initially saw exactly what they were saying. There are several scriptures which seem to prohibit women from leadership. For example, *"Women shall keep silent in the church; for they are not permitted to speak."*[1] And, *"I permit not a woman to teach or have authority over a man."*[2]

I would question scriptures like this regarding the women issue only so I could fully grasp and understand the church's position. It was not that I did not believe them—I just wanted to understand why and how to apply them. However, I was often met with strong, almost venomous, reactions. You would have thought I was questioning the validity and power of the cross. It was clear I was wading into shark-infested waters. However, I was willing to accept their interpretation and even prove their case to others,

[1] 1 Corinthians 14:34
[2] 1 Timothy 2:12

if I could fully comprehend it. My questioning was not to be rebellious but rather so I could truly make the Biblical position my own. In the beginning, if pressed, my answer would

> My questioning was not to be rebellious but rather so I could truly make the Biblical position my own.

have been that women are to be silent and are not to have key roles of authority because the Bible says so. My heart just wanted to understand why.

The Lord changed my answer when He asked me one simple question. He turned me around on a dime. I cannot give you the exact day, but it was still pretty early in my walk. I had just dropped the kids off at school, pulled back in the garage, and had gotten out of my car. I was heading toward the kitchen door when I heard the Lord ask me a question. I remember exactly where I was when the Lord spoke to me. It was not an audible, external voice. It was subtle enough that I could have missed it. Yet, there was no way I could have dismissed it! It was the Lord speaking. I just knew.

I heard Him ask, "Susan, why would I send Mary to tell the disciples knowing they would not believe her?" Wow. If it was not right for women to teach or deliver new revelation to men, then why would Jesus have sent Mary Magdalene to the male disciples with the greatest, most important revelation ever spoken: "He is risen!"? Why would He do that? Holy moly! He was alive! He was no longer lying dead in the grave! It was the single most important announcement ever uttered! It was the greatest message ever delivered! Jesus specifically chose a woman first to deliver the message of His resurrection. Why? Why would He send Mary to give that message to a group of grown men, especially considering that He knew that they would not believe her?

I had never given that question a thought—but Jesus had. He knew full well the disciples would not believe her, and yet He sent her anyway. At the core, His question to me was, "Why would I do that?"

With His voice comes a knowing—a revelation, an understanding, even a peace. Somehow, I just knew He wanted me to see that it was okay for a woman to deliver this amazing message. He had intentionally chosen her to do so. God was also communicating to me that what I currently believed about women was wrong. This one question began to challenge and to change my thinking.

Please understand it was not *the question*, "Why would I send Mary?", as much as it was *the fact that He was asking*. He was prompting me to question my beliefs! He was setting me up to go on a mission and a journey with Him. He does that, you know! He just sets us up in a beautiful way.

As I am standing in the garage, my mind is thinking, "Okay, now I clearly know God's heart! I'm going to go in the house, open up my Bible, pull out some Greek lexicons, and find the proof that we have it all wrong." I thought it was going to be really simple to show myself, and then others, where we had messed up our interpretation of God's Word on the subject. After all, God just spoke to me!

I went in the house, opened my Bible, and looked up all the relevant scriptures, cross references, definitions, you name it—hoping to find some evidence to prove what I now knew in my heart to be true. I now understood that God's heart did not match my theology. The problem was I could not find the smoking gun, at least not at first.

First Corinthians 14:34 plainly says, "*Women are to keep silent in church; for they're not permitted to speak.*" As I looked up the Greek words, I realized my effort to prove God's heart was going downhill fast. The word for "silent" in this verse is the Greek verb *sigao*. It means to be or to become silent, or to be hidden or concealed. The word for "speak" is the Greek word *laleo*, which means to speak or to talk. So twice in this one verse it seems to clearly state that women are not to have sound come out of their mouth in church. It appears that the text is literally saying, "women are not permitted to have any sound coming out of their mouth in church—no sound at all!" Be silent, hidden, concealed, and do not speak. That is clear, is it not?

Further, it is not just that they cannot teach or give their opinion. The following verse says women are not even to ask a question in church. *Not even ask a question!* From where I was sitting, things just went from bad to worse.

Processing this with the Lord, I questioned,

> I began to
> wonder why we
> let women sing
> in the choir?

"Okay, I know in my heart what You are saying to me, but what I'm seeing in your Word looks even more restrictive! Women are not even permitted to make any sound in church?! No sound at all... not even ask a question? Seriously?!"

I began to wonder, why do we allow women to sing in the choir? Singing is sound coming out of the mouth. That is not being silent. Why were we letting them lead worship or teach young children—teach *young* children? In many churches, women are restricted from teaching, based on the verse in 1 Timothy 2:14, which appears to say women can be deceived and get off into error (just like what happened at the fall with Eve). If that were true, and God wanted us to restrict women because they are more easily deceived, then why would we allow them to teach the young and impressionable (who may not recognize error) but not teach the older and wiser (who should know better)? Additionally, why would we allow them to teach other women (who are more easily deceived) but not teach the men (who should more readily recognize error). None of that made any logical sense whatsoever.

I began to see our application of these admonitions was irrational. Proof of the selective application could be seen in that my church did not require us to wear head coverings, yet in 1 Corinthians 11:6, it clearly states, with the same apparent vigor as in Chapter 14, that women must cover their head while praying or prophesying. I am definitely not sure how that was supposed to be done without the women making a sound. It further states that the head covering was a symbol of submission to authority. Again, I took all this to God. "Lord, I will do whatever it is You want me to do, and I will honor You. I will cover my head if You want me to, but this just does not make any sense at all. Please help me to understand Your heart."

I believe His Word and I trust His heart. I truly would cover my head for Jesus if I thought that is what He wanted me to do. I really would!

I was completely embroiled in this struggle to figure out how and why we selectively apply these verses. Why do we allow women to uncover their heads, but yet we do not allow them to teach adult men? Why pick one restrictive verse but not the other? If the restrictions were merely cultural or for that time period only, then today's western world churches would no longer prohibit women from teaching—just like they no longer require their heads to be covered in public. However, in many churches today, prohibitions against the female gender not only exist but are also strongly espoused because it is believed to be the will of God.

Thus began my long journey of searching. There was a vast chasm between what I knew to be God's heart and what I saw in His word. That chasm did not exist in reality, just in my understanding. I went on a quest to find where I was wrong. I read books

> Femininity is not a character deficit…

and articles; I studied the Word, and I even called a number of different ministries to ask them about the basis for their varying positions regarding women in ministry. I do not mind telling you, it was a frustrating trip. It took me six years to get from that initial starting point to knowing confidently I could prove what I thought God said to me in the garage was indeed His heart—that it is okay for Him to send women. I can assure you it is! In fact, women are a key in the establishment of His Kingdom on earth. This book will present the foundation of what I learned. The *Crown Her a King* series will demonstrate the evidence which proves that case.

God did not create the female to play a merely secondary, assistant-type role. Nor is there anything innate in women that caused the fall. Women can be trusted with truth. Femininity is not a character deficit, it is part of God's design for humanity. It is also necessary for human leadership in the Church to reflect the full image of God. That requires both masculine and feminine attributes to be fully present and honored.

Everything God does has a purpose, and Jesus sent Mary for a reason. He was shaking up the old mindset that believed women could not be trusted with revelation. In the culture of that day, He should have sent a man to proclaim the greatest message ever delivered. Yet He did not, and He did it that way on purpose. Many in Christendom today still believe God created the woman as a gift to the man. This so twists and perverts God's purposes that individual destinies are diminished and even destroyed. Worse yet, the manifestation of God's Kingdom is weak on the earth.

The issue of the woman's role in the Church is not a distraction, and it is not a secondary issue. Not only is the power of God's Kingdom on earth hindered by our lack of unity, but the secular world dismisses us as irrelevant because of it. It does not take a degree in theology or even faith in Jesus to know that any form of bigotry is wrong. It is confusing to preach a God of love and male chauvinism. The women issue is a primary source of the Church's lack of influence in our culture today. God is opening eyes and hearts to the truth that in Christ there is neither male nor female. We are all one in Him, and He is calling us to unite and advance His Kingdom. Unless we honestly confront our own twisted theology and irrational application of scripture on this subject, we will not experience the full manifestation of the power of His Word.

Do not be scared off by the radical call of this book. Just because you were always taught something, or just because everyone else you know believes it, does not make it true. Today we have no doubt that the earth is round. When I was in school, I was taught that for much of human history the uneducated masses believed that the earth was flat. From what I was taught, that notion remained common until the

1400 and 1500s when Christopher Columbus, Ferdinand Magellan, and other pioneers began making trips across the ocean. In hindsight, we can point to Isaiah 40:22, "It is He who sits above the *circle of the earth*." God's Word never claimed a flat earth but a round one. The book of Isaiah had been around for 2,200 years before Magellan ever set sail. Do not be foolish enough to continue to believe something just because it is a popular theory. Test the Word, and prove God's faithfulness and truth for yourself.

Would you like to know how we got the women issue so wrong to start with? You will be shocked at how it happened.

Three

She has *Chaldee*!

At the beginning of 2006, I moved from Maryland to Texas. The following year I had a dream while on a trip visiting back east. I am not normally a big dreamer. I am more of a studier. I am a left-brain, analytical type that enjoys looking up definitions and processing things logically. That is my norm. Dreams are unusual for me. If they grip me and stay with me, then I know it is God. While I was back east I had this powerful, heart-stopping dream. It was very simple and very short. As I awoke out of a dead sleep, my heart was racing and my whole body was sweating; I was literally panicked!

Before we pursue my dream, let me give you a little background. At the time I had two dogs, a pair of Dobermans named Priscilla and Aquila after the famous husband and wife teaching team mentioned in four New Testament books.[3] Over these years, I had developed a burning desire to preach, to teach, and to write—but I still was unclear what my role could be because of my gender. In hindsight, I suppose naming my female dog Priscilla was a prophetic act of faith. We got her first. If Priscilla in the Bible could teach then perhaps so could I. A couple of years later, Aquila joined our family. Even though I saw lots of pro-female verses and examples in the scriptures, I could not shake off the negative ones. How could I violate something that was clearly written

---

[3] Priscilla (Prisca) and Aquila: See Acts 18:2, 18, 26, Romans 16:3, 1 Corinthians 16:19, 2 Timothy 4:19

She's not okay! She has *CHALDEE!*

in the Bible, there in black and white, even though I knew God was trying to tell me something different? Amidst the confusion, I was reluctant to move forward until I could biblically answer the question, "How free am I?"

In my dream, Priscilla (a.k.a. Prissy) was in some kind of an institutional building. I do not know exactly what it was, but it was a large building. Just inside the lobby there was a counter. Behind it stood a woman wearing a white lab coat as if she was official—definitely part of the institution. In the dream, I was so upset with this woman. She was holding a medical clipboard with Prissy's chart on it. I could clearly see that there was a problem, but she was acting as if everything was fine.

At the bottom of the clipboard was written "C-H-A-L-D-E-E" in huge three or four inch letters. I was pointing at the clipboard shouting, "No! No! No! It is not okay! **She is not okay! She has** *CHALDEE***!"** However, the woman just stood there looking at me with this mannequin-like, Stepford-wife-like oblivious smile, as if to say, "Everything's okay. Everything's fine." However, it was not even close to *fine*! She was completely blind to the fact that there was a serious, even catastrophic, problem. I remember waking up with my heart beating out of my chest. I immediately asked God, "What was that? What are You trying to tell me? And what in the world does *Chaldee* mean?"

The dream just haunted me. I could not get those images of the woman's face and the clipboard with

> "...Christian woman has *Chaldee*."

CHALDEE out of my head. Nor could I shake the overwhelming sense that something was terribly wrong. Later, while visiting some friends, I shared the dream hoping to get an interpretation. One person quickly knew by the Spirit that Priscilla meant Christian woman. That totally rang true in my spirit—my baby jumped. Have you ever heard that expression? "My baby jumped," meaning my spirit leapt. I just knew she was right; Priscilla meant Christian woman.

It seemed that God was telling me, "Christian woman has *Chaldee*." This did not really help me understand any better. "Who is the Christian woman? Is it me? Is it someone else? Is it all Christian women? And what in the world does *Chaldee* mean?" My first reaction was to do my normal left-brain, pull out the concordances, and do all the intellectual study stuff. Here is what I found. *Chaldee* was the language of the Chaldeans, and Abraham came out of the city Ur, which was in Chaldea. I made that connection, but I still had no idea what "Christian woman has *Chaldee*" could possibly mean.

I also did not understand why I was so upset. Seriously, without even knowing yet what *Chaldee* was, my heart was seriously troubled. I knew the message of the dream was significant, and I knew it was very

> I often found that the spirits behind both sides of the debate were coming from the wrong kingdom.

important to God that I grasp what it meant. Yet at that point in time, I simply could not get any further clarification.

After returning to Texas, I "coincidentally" signed up for a course through Christian Leadership University online entitled, "God's Release of Women". If you have never heard of Mark Virkler or his books *How to Hear God's Voice* or *Dialogue with God*, I strongly recommend them. I wish every new-believer's class used them because so many Christians walk through life struggling to hear God. Too often, we do not recognize nor honor the Voice of the One we profess to serve. Mark and his wife, Patty, are the directors of Christian Leadership University.[4]

Prior to taking this course, I always felt uncomfortable when studying the women issue. No matter which side I was currently looking at, it seemed like something was always wrong. Too often, the arguments were circular in nature. One poor fellow I read even argued that since God created two genders, male and female, then that alone proves there could not be equality between the sexes. He surmised, since there are two, one must be above the other. Is that godly? Does that fit with your vision of the Kingdom of Heaven? Sadly, while researching, I often found

---

[4]http://www.cluonline.com

44

that the spirits behind both sides of the debate were coming from the wrong kingdom. After reading their arguments, I would usually be left feeling like I needed to take a spiritual shower.

On one hand, I would read authors who had a more traditional interpretation. They taught that women are not supposed to lead based on their gender. They believe the Bible teaches that women were created to be man's helper; therefore, they are always supposed to be in a submissive, supportive, non-leadership role. Additionally, they support their case with a few verses in scripture that appear very prohibitory toward women. These traditionalists (or "complementarians" as many preferred to be called) do not believe women are less valuable in their personhood, but certainly they are to be secondary in their position. In their estimation, since women were meant to be an assistant by God's design, therefore it is unbiblical and wrong for women to lead or to teach men.

However, this seemed contrary to other scriptures which declare, *"In Christ there is no male and female"*[5] or that both *"your sons and your daughters would prophesy."*[6] Not to mention the fact that Paul wrote about women in ministry throughout his letters. Whenever I would read the more traditional authors, I knew something was terribly wrong, but I could not put my finger on exactly what it was.

However, as I noted earlier, when I would read the arguments of the opposing, pro-female side, I also felt that something was not right. Often the

[5] Galatians 3:28
[6] Acts 2:17, quoting Joel 2:28

authors were very hostile, very bitter. Some would dismiss Paul's words because they deemed him wrong on the subject. Others would claim they were only culturally relevant for Paul's day and time, and therefore those scriptures were not applicable today. I felt very uncomfortable with both of those positions because Paul wrote two-thirds of the New Testament. If he was wrong or if his words were only for early church, then why would God have included them in the Bible?

I was embroiled in this inner struggle for six years, with neither side giving me satisfactory answers. Finally, while I am taking this class from Christian Leadership University, the light began to dawn. Guess what I found out? One of the first things the Lord highlighted to me was *CHALDEE*. Hang with me here as I explain what that means because this will fundamentally shift everything.

When the Jews were exiled into Babylon, they wrote down their oral traditions so they would not lose their Jewish culture even though they were living in captivity in a foreign land. That was a great plan, really. No matter where they ended up geographically or into what society they were assimilated, by keeping hold of their traditions they would forever remain Jewish. They would rehearse their past, continue with their customs, teach their doctrines, and keep their ethnicity. They would never lose their Jewish identity, even after generations of living outside of their homeland. They could still be 'Jewish' no matter where they resided. History later proved how vital this was, because their nation was able to survive without a homeland for nearly two thousand years!

Looking all the way back to the beginning of

> …the Jewish males would start their day by thanking God that they were "not born a gentile, a woman, or an ignoramus."

the Hebrew nation, remember father Abraham was called out of the Chaldean city of Ur. He was led by God to the Promised Land. If you compare a few historical maps, you will notice that Ur was located in the southern part of the Euphrates and Tigris river region. Later, this whole region became part of the Babylonian Empire. Fifteen hundred years after Abraham left the pagan world system to follow God's voice, his descendants would be taken captive and exiled back to this very region. Because of the hardness of their hearts, they were exiled from the Promised Land and were enslaved in Babylon.

It was here that many of the Jewish oral traditions were written down and codified. What struck me was that when the Jews recorded their cultural norms, many anti-female sentiments were included in them. For example, the Jewish males would start their day by thanking God that they were "not born a gentile, a woman, or an ignoramus." In these documents, there is actually a discussion about dropping the word 'ignoramus' and replacing it with 'slave.' However, the discussion points out that to thank God that they

> The language in which the Talmud was originally written is commonly termed Chaldee.

were not born a 'slave' would be redundant. They already thanked God that they were not born a woman, and since females were doomed to a life of servitude to males, thanking Him they were not born as slaves would be repetitious. Since women lived a life of slavery, thanking God that they were not born a woman was already thanking Him that they were not slaves. They were right; indeed it would be repetitive. This is sad but true. Many of these ancient writings are included in the Talmud, which is still read today.

You may be asking, "So what?" Hang with me because getting this point is important to the foundation of the entire *Crown Her a King* series.

"The language of the Talmud is commonly termed *Chaldee*."[7] *Chaldee* is Eastern Aramean, from the Babylon province occupying the Euphrates and Tigris river region.[8] It was this language that the exiled Jews learned while being held captive to the world power that enslaved them. These anti-female sentiments were actually written down in the ancient language of *Chaldee—C-H-A-L-D-E-E*! My dream was beginning to make sense!

---

[7] Riggs, Elias DD, and Georg Benedikt Winer, _A Manual of the Chaldee Language_. (New York: Anson D.F. Randolf and Co., 900 Broadway, Cor. 20th Street), 1858. Page 13, note 2. See also, _Cyclopaedia of Biblical, Theological, and Ecclesiastical Literature_, Vol II, C-D, by John McClintock and James Strong. (New York: Harper & Brothers, Publishers, Franklin Square), 1894. Page 201.

[8] Riggs, _A Manual of the Chaldee Language_, page 9.

The Talmud is a wonderful historical document, important for the Jewish culture, and I mean it no disrespect. It is vital, however, that we grasp the fact that many of these oral traditions were codified in Babylon. In the Old Testament, Babylon is a type or shadow of the world systems which oppose God's Kingdom. Similarly early on in God's story, Egypt was a type or shadow of the world apart from His domain. We read in Exodus of how God miraculously delivered His people out of Egypt through Moses. You know the story of the ten plagues and the parting of the Red Sea. God delivered His people out of bondage, out of slavery to the world's system, and He set them apart to be His people in the Promised Land.

What did this have to do with my dream? God was driving home the point that Babylon represents the world outside His Kingdom, outside the Promised Land, where His people are once again enslaved. It was the same world that the father of our faith was called to come out from. However, that world was once again infecting the hearts and minds of God's people.

Sadly, even though these anti-female sentiments originated in the world—in the wrong kingdom—they have woven themselves into the fabric of the Judeo-Christian culture. After the Jews codified their oral traditions, they became official. These dark, evil thoughts had infiltrated and imprisoned God's women. Take for example the Talmudic "Ten Curses of Eve", which include among other things, women having to cover their heads "like a mourner" and "living a life

> The dream meant that Christian women had been poisoned by satan through the traditions of the world outside the Kingdom of God.

of domestic imprisonment."

This is not God's will. It was evil's influence upon the world's systems, then fully embraced and legally codified by God's chosen. The enemy had seduced mankind to desire power and control over each other, even to the extreme point of enslaving one's own family. **Bondage at any level is the antithesis of freedom; it is the antithesis of love, and it is the antithesis of God's Kingdom.** "Where the Spirit of the Lord is there is freedom."[9] Where evil reigns, freedom is suppressed.

When I learned that these traditions had been formalized and codified in *Chaldee*—in the language of the world outside God's Kingdom—I began to weep. God had clearly spoken in my dream. Now there was no longer any doubt whatsoever. That dream prepared my heart to receive what He was getting ready to reveal to me. My heart was open and ready for Him to teach me His truth.

The dream meant that Christian women had been poisoned by satan through the traditions of the world outside the Kingdom of God. **"She has *Chaldee*" meant the entire Church was infected.** This poison spread like a cancer and was perpetuated by those

---

[9] 2 Corinthians 3:17 (New International Version), "Now the Lord is the Spirit, and where the Spirit of the Lord is, there is freedom."

who were "teaching as doctrines the precepts of men."[10] The word for 'men' here does not mean 'male', it means 'human'. It is the Greek word *anthrōpos*.[11]

> ...anti-female sentiments had come from the world outside God's Kingdom, not from God's Word.

So many times, we think the Bible is saying 'males' when it is simply saying 'humans'. The "precepts of men"[12] are commandments, directives, rules of conduct, and guides made from worldly, fleshly thinking as opposed to being precepts from God.

Through the dream, Holy Spirit was highlighting that these anti-female sentiments had come from the world outside God's Kingdom, not from God's Word. This was an evil cancer poisoning His people—but most Christians are blind to it, just like the woman in my dream standing behind the counter wearing the white lab coat. What happens to a body with cancer if it goes unnoticed and therefore untreated? It becomes malignant, eating away and destroying God's beautiful creation.

These anti-female sentiments did not begin with the Talmud or *Chaldee*—clearly they have been around since the fall of man. By the time of the Babylonian captivity, these anti-female "women were created to serve men" type ideas had become so accepted, they were documented and codified as if they

---

[10] Matthew 15:9
[11] *anthrōpos*, human being, Strong's #G444
[12] Mark 7:7, See also Isaiah 29:13-14

were, in fact, the will of God! Even God's chosen people had been infected with this evil, malignant cancer from the world. It did not stop with the Jewish nation. For centuries, Christ's Church has been blind to the malevolent force eating away at the inside of Her.

There is no doubt that this cancer is still alive in the Bride of Christ today. It truly is a catastrophic problem! No wonder my spirit had been so troubled by the dream. The exposure of this "cancerous *Chaldee*" was a huge revelation! Like going to the doctor after being sick for a long time, knowing there is as a problem but not knowing what was wrong. Then comes the revelation—the diagnosis—it is cancer!

The illness that has infected the Church is almost too huge to comprehend. I would be discouraged and overwhelmed if I did not know that God Himself is actively and strategically working to remove this cancer from His Body. Only after the diagnosis—only after acknowledging that there is a problem—can treatment and healing begin.

Five hundred years after the Jews returned from captivity to their homeland in Israel, God became man and walked among us. In Jesus' day, the scribes and Pharisees revered these Talmudic traditions and doctrines of men. They would memorize and quote them, holding them on almost equal par with the scriptures. In this culture, women were not permitted to speak in public, not even to their husbands— and especially not if he was a rabbi. If a woman was to pass by her husband in public, she was to remain silent. If she spoke to him publically, that would dishonor him. Can you imagine that? Women were not allowed even to speak to their own husband in public!

This type of treatment of women was not confined to Israel. In varying degrees, this was a worldwide epidemic. In that region of the world, women still continue to be severely oppressed. Even today in the twenty-first century, Muslim women of certain sects and in certain countries are not allowed to have a driver's license, be educated, uncover their head, or go out in public without a male family member chaperone.

> Jesus never sinned, yet He violated the man-made customs of His day by chatting with *the woman at the well.*

Jesus is perfect theology. I love how He graciously treated women despite the harsh culture of His day. As we venture deeper into this series, you will see women in the Bible in ministry you probably never even noticed before. Did you know there are over 180 women named in the Bible? Not to mention many others like Noah's wife or the woman at the well whose names were never recorded.

Jesus never sinned, yet He violated the manmade customs of His day by chatting with the woman at the well. According to their cultural mandates, she was not allowed to talk to men in public, but Jesus was the one who started the conversation. To compound the matter, she was a Samaritan—a mixed race hated by the Jews. Later, when His disciples returned from getting food, it was her gender that shocked them not her heritage. They could not believe Jesus was having a conversation with a woman.

> *At this point His disciples came, and **they were amazed that He had been speaking with a woman**, yet no one said, "What do You seek?" or, "Why do You speak with her?"*
>
> John 4:27

These manmade traditions were taught as if they were doctrines from God, but they were not. If this had been a godly restriction, Jesus would have upheld it. He fulfilled the law perfectly, going so far as to be baptized in water even though He did not need to be. Jesus did not need to be baptized for the remissions of sins because He was sinless. When John the Baptist protested, "Jesus answering said to him, 'Permit it at this time; for in this way it is fitting for us to fulfill all righteousness.'"[13] Meaning, He wanted to obey all the godly precepts, even the ones that did not necessarily apply to Him. He wanted to do all the right things— all acts of righteousness. If the restriction against women speaking to men outside their home was of God, then Jesus would have upheld it.

In Matthew chapter 15 and Mark chapter 7, Jesus calls out the scribes and Pharisees for treating these traditions and doctrines of men like they were the word of God. By doing this they were rendering

---

[13] Matthew 3:15

God's Word of no effect, making it void of power, even nullifying it.[14] If you mix water into your gasoline, your car will not run. Even the most pious and religious people of His day had unknowingly been mixing worldly, human precepts into God's doctrines making them powerless.

> ...Jesus calls out the scribes and Pharisees for treating these traditions and doctrines of men like they were the word of God.

Paul's writings are in fact scripture, so please hear me. The Talmudic and other oral traditions are not the inspired word of God; they are man's precepts—some are wonderful, some are in error. Paul's writings in the New Testament are never in error; they are the inspired Word of God. Please do not confuse what I'm saying: The Bible, and what Paul says in it, is scripture and should be revered as such. It is God's Word. It is 100% accurate, and we can trust it implicitly. It is our plumb line. The Word of God is without error, but our interpretation of it is not.

Each of the difficult, seemingly female-restrictive verses in the Bible will be dealt with during this series. What you learn will blow you away! How all this fits together is earth shattering! It is amazing! I promise

---

[14]Mark 7:13, "And so you cancel the word of God in order to hand down your own tradition. And this is only one example among many others." (New Living Translation). "Making the word of God of no effect through your tradition which you have handed down...", (New King James Version). See also Matthew 15:1-9, and Mark 7:1-13

whether you are male or female, you will be liberated! The truth about God's Kingdom, and how we all (male and female) fit into it, will revolutionize your life!

Four

Faulty Filters

As I was taking the class, "God's Release of Women," Holy Spirit revealed so many amazing truths. What I had previously understood about what the Bible said regarding the topic of women in ministry was completely wrong, or at least my interpretation of it was all wrong. God did not make any mistakes when He gave us the scriptures, even though He did so through human vessels. However, not all interpretations are inspired. Here is the problem: When you have a filter on, whatever you see is affected by that filter. Because you think a certain way, or when you believe something to be inherently true, then whenever you look at it, you only see what you expect to see. Does that make sense?

This may help clarify. Lance Wallnau,[15] a well-known executive business coach and speaker, offered a live example of this phenomenon. In a room filled with Christian leaders, he unveiled a large number of different colored objects on the stage. He gave them a few seconds to count how many yellow objects were present. He covered the objects again and asked, "Now tell me how many purple objects were present?" The leaders were frustrated and confused. They could not answer his question because they only saw what they looked for. They looked only for the yellow. They did not know how many purple objects were present because they did not see them.

---

[15] http://www.lancelearning.com/

> The restriction of women is a faulty filter.

They only had knowledge regarding the number of yellow because that is what they focused on. They only saw what they expected to see.

If you already believe the scriptures say that women cannot be in positions of leadership or teach adult men, then that is all you will most likely see when you look at the Word. You are confined by your filter, and your interpretation is often formulated by how you were taught to look at it. The premise that the Bible teaches any form of discrimination based on gender is in error. The restriction of women is a faulty filter. It is an interpretation that is just not true.

Gain with me a sense and an understanding of both where we are currently and where we are going. Right now, the world is fallen. It is dark. It is weak, and it is divided. Right? Sadly, the church is not much better off. However, in the beginning, in the Garden of Eden, God's original plan was for a world very different from what we live in now. What He created was a paradise filled with intimacy, beauty, abundance, and life: not division, evil, poverty, toil, pain, and sickness—not even death. The Garden was created to be a place of love, unity, and proper dominion. After God spoke the world into being and formed the animals, He turned His attention toward the pinnacle of His creation, mankind, and He said this:

Let Us make man in Our image, according to

Our likeness; and let them rule over the fish of the sea and over the birds of the sky and over the cattle and over all the earth, and over every creeping thing that creeps on the earth." God created man in His own image, in the image of God He created him; male and female He created them.

Genesis 1:26-27

Here is the point: God made humans *In His Image*. Notice the plural pronouns God uses in describing Himself with regard to the creation of humanity. He says, "Let *Us* make man in *Our* image, according to *Our* likeness….."[16] Note again that the word 'man' here, like in Matthew 15, does not mean "male"; rather it means "human." It is the Hebrew word *adam*,[17] similar to the Greek word *anthrōpos*. We will discuss the gender distinctions further in the third book of this series, *Who's the Helper?* For now, it is important to see that God, who is plural, is making a human in that image.

God is a plural unity. There is the Father, the Son, and the Holy Spirit. They are distinctly different. Jesus is not the same as the Holy Spirit, who is not the same as the Father, and yet They are all ONE. "Hear O Israel! The Lord is our God, the Lord is one!"[18] That word for "one" is the Hebrew word *'echad*.[19] *'Echad* carries with it a more complex definition of one. In

---

[16] Genesis 1:26
[17] *'adam*, human, Strong's #H120
[18] Deuteronomy 6:4
[19] Strong's #H259

> Our emphasis then should be on our unity, our togetherness, not on our differences.

this case, it is a collective one, like one bunch of grapes. It is not the word *yachiyd*,[20] which would convey a simpler meaning like one singular, solitary grape. *'Echad* is greater than that. Our God is a plurality, composed of more than one, and yet the emphasis is on Their togetherness, Their oneness, Their unity. They may each be unique and different, but They are still one.

We commonly refer to all three of the Godhead together as the "Trinity." That term is not in the Bible, but it is a great word to describe all three as one. The Father, Son, and Holy Spirit are three distinct entities, but the emphasis here in the creation account is on Their togetherness not on Their individuality. It says, "let US make...;" not, "I'll make this part and You make that...." As Christians, we are monotheists. We believe in one God: Father, Son and Holy Spirit. When God created humans, He created us in His image to be plural and yet one. **Our emphasis then should be on our unity, our togetherness, not on our differences.**

God's plan from the beginning was for male and female to be a plural unity, as He is a plural unity. We seem to ignore that God has both masculine and feminine characteristics. Now, He is Spirit,[21] not flesh and blood, so He is neither male nor female. It takes

---

[20] Stong's #H3173

[21] "Now the Lord is the Spirit...." (2 Corinthians 3:17a)

60

both genders to reflect His image. For example, He is both a warrior and a comforter. He is a provider and a nurturer. In the Garden there was to be both intimacy and action. It was not all romance and gardening.

The mandate was not just to cultivate the Garden, it was also to "keep" it.[22] The Hebrew word here for "keep" is *shamar,*[23] which means to guard and protect. If part of the mandate was to guard and protect, then that means there was indeed an enemy. From the beginning, mankind needed to be ready to do battle. The fight would not just be defensive in nature, but it would need to be offensive as well. The Lord commanded them to take dominion and subdue the earth. Clearly, as part of the original design, there was both relationship and adventure to be experienced.

There is no absolute clear delineation between femininity and masculinity, yet we seem inherently to know the difference. Just as one example, women tend to be more sensitive and relational, while men tend to be stronger and more adventuresome. That does not mean men are not sensitive or relational, nor does that mean women are not strong or adventuresome. It just seems that the genders are wired with different emphases.

It takes both the male and the female to reflect fully God's glory and His image on the earth. It takes both men and women to reveal God's attributes to those who do not know Him. We can only fully reflect who He is to the world when we come

[22] Genesis 2:15
[23] *Shamar,* Strong's H8104

together, never when we divide! The main point of "Let Us make man in Our image" is that they were plural yet one. Therefore, our God-given glory and power are only manifested in our unity, never in our divisions.

We reflect the beauty of the Trinity when we join together with our differences being the very place of our union—like puzzle pieces that fit perfectly together. In marriage, a husband and wife physically join together at the place where their bodies are different. This is also true in the realms of the soul and the spirit. We will dive deeper into this in Book Nine, *United We Stand*.... However, it is vitally important while building the foundation for this series, that we comprehend it is at the point of our God-given differences that we are supposed to come together.

These differences can be as simple as logical vs. creative or people-oriented vs task-oriented. We are all gifted and wired differently. As individuals, we are unique; there is not one other exactly like us. We will have similarities with others based on our genetics, passion, gifting, culture, race, gender... you name it. If we are not careful, we will see those most like ourselves as better than the others.

Our differences are intended to be the places where we connect, but they have been used as the basis for our divisions. Since the fall of man, the enemy has been able to influence our thinking. What God meant to bind, the enemy used to splinter. **The enemy twists the truth so our differences end up being the very things we divide over.**

Can you see one picture here with two different points of view? In God's eyes, the differences are meant to be the very places of our

> ...the enemy's strategy was to tear the man and woman apart.

connection. The twisted perspective sees our differences as points of separation or disconnection. In the Garden, the man and woman were created to be *one* in God's image. Therefore, the enemy's strategy was to tear the man and woman apart. That is exactly what happened. The couple believed the lie and ate the forbidden fruit. The results were catastrophic as fear replaced relationship. Shame replaced security, and blame replaced unity. The enemy successfully drove a wedge between the first couple.

Instead of standing side-by-side subduing the earth together, we turned and began to rule one another—first through the sexes, then through the races and economic classes—with whatever division God's enemy could get us to justify or tolerate. Instead of dispelling the darkness, we make agreement with it. He wants us to dominate one another for this is how he wins. He knows we will never be able to conquer him as long as we are divided—as long as our original glory is torn and tattered.

We humans yielded our rightful dominion over the earth and over the enemy ("let them rule"[24]). Instead, people sought to dominate other people. It got so twisted and ingrained in our thinking, that now we

---

[24]Genesis 1:26

> We lost sight of God's original plan, and then we forgot who we were supposed to be in it.

believe this kind of hierarchy is customary and even godly. Power struggles are felt at every level of society, permeating every area of our culture. It is even in the church world and viewed as normal. We overlay the power pyramid into our leadership structure, thinking it is the only option available.

We lost sight of God's original plan, and then we forgot who we were supposed to be in it. That is why the *Crown Her a King* series deals directly with issues like establishing God's Kingdom on earth, taking dominion in our everyday lives, and discovering our true identity as royal priests. If we are ever going to be restored to the original, glorious image of oneness, then men and women alike need to become all that God intended them to be, both individually and corporately. We all need to know how to rule nobly, yielding to the voice of the Lord.

The *Crown Her a King* series is bigger than the women issue. The women issue is key, however, because the Church has been poisoned with *Chaldee*. Poisoned! The whole Church is sick, not just the females! This is a cancer that has kept the Bride under satan's feet. If one half of a couple's glory is veiled or power restricted, then neither of them can function properly. **The effects are exponential!**

If you have a car and half of it is broken, how well

does the other half operate? Does it operate at half capacity? No! At best it may be creeping along, but more likely it would be dead in a junk yard. It is one car. You cannot expect it to operate if half of it is broken. That is not how it was engineered.

> Male and female were created to be different parts of one powerful unit.

That is not how we were designed either. Male and female were created to be different parts of one powerful unit. Yet the world has not seen such a powerful team walk the earth, at least not since the Garden. All of creation is still waiting for us to grow up and become who and what God created and designed us to be. "For the anxious longing of the creation waits eagerly for the revealing of the sons of God."[25]

I am sure you guessed this, but "son" in this verse does not exclusively mean "male" child. The word can be used for boys, but it can be used for girls also. In context, the word is focusing on becoming mature children[26] as opposed to babies. The world is waiting for us to grow up enough to take our rightful place, destroying the enemy's evil influence over the world's systems. Since the fall, we have forgotten who we truly are. The entire creation suffers as it waits for us to awaken out of our confusion. We must understand all that we are in Christ!

Can you see now why the Church is weak and less

[25] Romans 8:19
[26] *Huios*, Strong's #G5207

influential than She should be? She is broken. She is sick! She has *CHALDEE*! It is time for things to change! God is clearly at work bringing healing to the Body with His message of freedom for women.

I am not the only Christian voice declaring equality and unity of the sexes. All throughout the United States and around the world, ministers are preaching and writing books on this very topic. I especially love the messages coming out of Bethel Church in Redding California. Kris Vallotton and Danny Silk have fully captured God's heart, and they declare truth with courage and clarity. I love all their books and audio messages. You will see me quote Kris Vallotton's teachings so much throughout this series that I call myself a groupie. I highly recommend all their stuff![27]

Even with so many other voices speaking on the women issue, *Crown Her a King* has some significant and unique revelatory keys. We all have important pieces of the puzzle. Most assuredly, with all of us on the message simultaneously, the entire Church is going to explode with new, healthy life because it is time. In the scope of human history, there has never been a more strategic time to pull back the curtain and reveal what has been cloaked in darkness. It is time to remove the faulty filters and see the truth as it has been from the beginning.

---

[27] Kris Vallotton has a number of audio messages available including, "*God's Most Beautiful Creation;*" "*God's Secret Weapon: Women;*" "*Jesus: The Founder of the Women's Liberation Movement;*" "*Matriarchal Leadership.*" His website is kvministries.com // Danny Silk's audio messages include, "*And They Were all Filled: Honoring our Women;*" "*The Invisible Ceiling.*" Danny has also just released his new book: "*Powerful and Free: Confronting the Glass Ceiling for Women in the Church.*" His website is lovingonpurpose.com. You can also order these items from the Bethel Church website (ibethel.org), Amazon.com, or any major book retailer.

Five

The Hearts of Men
are Now Ready

On the day the veil finally came off my eyes, I was reading in my study. My heart was open to the information from the Christian Leadership University class because God had prepared me ahead of time through the *Chaldee* dream. Although I would never just take anyone else's opinion as gospel, I now had an anticipation that I was going to learn something brand new. I was not disappointed! As I was reading Professor Joanne Krupp's book, *WOMAN: God's Plan Not Man's Tradition*,[28] it was as if a light bulb was turned on in my head. In dealing with the "women shall keep silent in the church" verse, Mrs. Krupp clearly explained that Paul was quoting false Corinthian teachers. She demonstrated how Paul himself went on to refute their chauvinistic position. What a revelation! Paul was refuting those female-restrictive statements, not authoring them! This information changed everything!

If you think I have lost my mind, I do not blame you. However, before you put this book down thinking it is in error, please consider the possibility that what you currently believe to be true may in fact be wrong. Despite popular opinion, the earth may indeed be round.

Ask the Lord for a new filter before reading on. If

---

[28] Krupp, Joanne. *Woman: God's Plan not Man's Tradition* (Salem, Oregon: Preparing the Way Publishers) 1999. Pages 79-83

you are excited by what you just read, then chances are you do not need one. Regardless, I encourage you to ask the Lord to wipe your lenses clean. We have all been tainted in one degree or another by false teaching on this subject matter. It has permeated every single culture, and no one has fully escaped the enemy's lies. Not me, and not you either. With the Lord's help, we can wipe our slate clean. We should start with a fresh perspective not assuming we already know what the Bible says.

I personally was undone when I realized how wrong I had been. When I first saw Paul's familiar words through my new filter, I cried my eyes out. After Paul quoted the chauvinistic statement "women are to keep silent in the church," then he immediately contradicted it. Weeping may seem like an extreme reaction, but the truth that Paul had never meant to silence women overwhelmed my emotions. How could we have not seen that before?!

Then the tears turned to anger. Through clenched teeth I asked, "Lord, for millennia men and women alike have believed that it was Your plan for women to be secondary. We thought it was Your will for women to restrict their voice and be submissive to the men. But God, if this was NOT Your plan, then how could You allow this to happen?!"

Then the dark reality of where those evil notions had led humanity sunk in. "Lord! Women have been physically, emotionally, and sexually abused—even enslaved—for thousands of years!" I had a strong sense that the insidious root behind much of that abuse is the belief that women are to be beneath the men. If there was not at least some truth to that belief, then how could the Lord

> "The hearts of men are now ready to receive the truth."

have allowed His Church to believe it as well. Our most basic interpretation of God's design for humanity included this paradigm. I had assumed it was part of God's plan but man perverted it. Now that light of truth was dawning on me. This had never been part of His plan.

I was more than mad; I was enraged when I realized that it was not part of His economy to silence or keep women in a secondary position. After all, He was God. Why did He allow women be placed in a subservient role if that was not His original intention? How could He allow the weaker sex to suffer such abuses over the centuries—over the millennia?! The belief in a godly hierarchical structure for men and women has affected every single household that ever existed! If this was not His intention, then how could He let that happen? How could He let that happen and still be all-powerful? How could He let that happen and still be good?

God did not answer my accusation, go figure, but He did speak to me very loudly and very clearly. He said, **"The hearts of men are now ready to receive the truth."** With that statement, a sense of peace and hope washed over me. The rage faded away. The tears dried up. At that moment, I still had no comprehension of how or why the centuries of abuse happened the way they did. However, I understood the message that He did not want me to dwell on the past. He wanted me to be forward thinking because the time was now right for Him to reveal His will and His plan. The time was right for Him to replace our faulty filters, for the hearts of men were now ready to receive His truth.

His statement took me on another five-year journey. It has been well over a decade since I began this quest. You see, that day in my study, I did not have a grid for understanding God's Kingdom. My thinking did not line up with His thinking at all. I was a very devout Christian, and I had become well acquainted with the Bible, but I had no clue about His Kingdom. As I began to realize that He wanted to crown "Her" a king ("Her" meaning Christ's Bride, the Church, along with the individual females within it), I did not even know what being a king in the Kingdom was supposed to look like.

I know that may sound odd, but my level of understanding regarding the Kingdom was very elementary. I thought God's Kingdom was like a distant Heaven; I thought it was a far off place. I did not know that it was God's will being done on earth—right here, right now. Jesus came to establish the Kingdom here, among us. He did not come preaching only the Gospel of Salvation. The redemption of mankind was indeed central to His mission, but His primary message was the "Gospel of the Kingdom." Everywhere He went, He talked about the "kingdom." His

parables often began with, "the Kingdom is like…."
Amazingly, there were times when He would heal
someone and say, "The Kingdom has come upon
you."[29] This was His pattern everywhere He went.
If you read Matthew alone, it seems like every page
is talking about the Kingdom of God or the Kingdom of Heaven. That was the foundation of His
message, and yet my mind had on the old filters of
the outside world mingled with my new religious
system. I did not comprehend the Kingdom reality He was restoring to the earth. Nor did I understand that He commissioned us to carry on His
work, encouraging us to do even greater things.[30]

Before the Father could release me to write *Crown
Her a King*, I had to learn about this Kingdom. That
was the focus of this five-year jaunt. Holy Spirit led
me on a journey of discovery that placed this revelation of the women issue into proper perspective
within His Kingdom context. Otherwise, I would
have failed miserably. This would be especially true
if I empowered women (by convincing the Church
we had been wrong with regard to their secondary
status) but did not bring an understanding of God's
Kingdom with it. It would have been fruitless. You
see we would have come up out of the ditch of male
supremacy, crossed over the road of truth, and ended
up in a different ditch of error on the other side. A
twisted truth is no truth at all. The truth about the
women issue must be understood in the context of
His Kingdom.

[29] Matthew 12:28. See also Luke 10:8-11
[30] John 14:12

> The truth is that God wants women to be fully empowered, equal, and united with men...

Truth is powerful. Jesus said, "I am the Truth."[31] He is the perfect representation of truth, truth personified. If anything goes against what He said or did by example then it is not true! Truth is also like a narrow, powerful road that actually takes you somewhere in the Kingdom. Similarly, electricity is carried in a conduit. Kingdom power is contained and released in truth. Therefore, when you are on this road, things happen and the miraculous becomes normal. When the Kingdom is being manifest, God's will being done is a present reality. All the enemy needs to do to limit you is to get you off that road of truth and into a ditch. He does not care which ditch you fall into, so long as you are off that powerful road of truth.

The truth is that God wants women to be fully empowered, equal, and united with men, with their differences complementing one other. Only together can we reflect the image of the Godhead on the earth. We were made in His likeness as a plural unity. God spoke the world into being, then formed us in His image with a creative, powerful voice. If we believe that women should be silent or kept separate, especially from influence and decision-making, then we have fallen into a powerless ditch. We have fallen victim to the enemy's greatest scheme.

---

[31] John 14:6

72

Throughout human history, and still in many churches today, people believe women should not have a voice; they should not teach nor

> ...the enemy has successfully silenced the crowning jewel of creation.

have authority over adult men. This is the poisonous trench of male supremacy. It is here that the enemy successfully silenced the crowning jewel of creation. He stole both her voice and her freedom! Since men and women are divided, the devil has also robbed the Church of Her God-given power and glory.

On the flip side, some bitterly believe that the historical mistreatment of the feminine gender deserves retribution. In other words, they owe us. This is buying into yet another lie from the spirit of entitlement. To compound the matter, a large percentage of women today not only have domestic and parental duties, but they also carry the additional burden of solely providing for their families. Many end up as single moms, or worse, they choose abortion because the thought of raising children on their own is overwhelming.

Today, for children fortunate enough to be born, nearly half will be raised in a single parent household. According to the 2010 US Census, 85% of single-parent households are headed by women (11.9 million single parent households: 9.9 million are custodial moms, 1.8 million custodial dads).[32] Some of these

---

[32] In 1980, 18.4% of children were born to unmarried women. In 2008, that statistic is nearing half – 40.6%!! Page viewed 01-07-2012.

> This pattern is not only destroying the family, it is also destroying the fabric of our American society...

single parent homes are due to death or divorce, but a rapidly growing phenomenon is for father and mother never to marry. Since the 1980s, the rate of unmarried women having children has skyrocketed from 18.4% to nearly half—40.6%![33] Forty percent of all children born in the US right now are being born into homes where the father and mother never married.

This pattern is not only destroying the family, it is also destroying the fabric of our American society by creating a culture of poverty. In 2011, the Witherspoon Institute published an article, "The Two-Biological-Parent Family and Economic Prosperity: What's Gone Wrong."[34] This paper demonstrates the correlation between the decline of the U.S. economy and the rise of single parent households. Tragically, these children have become the victims of the spirit of poverty with 66% of them living below the poverty line. Comparatively, only 10% of children with two parents at home fall into that same category. "Since the rates of single-parenthood have risen so greatly, the largest proportion of the poor is no longer the elderly, but children."[35]

[33] Ibid.
[34] Jeynes, William, "The Two-Biological-Parent Family and Economic Prosperity: What's Gone Wrong": http://www.thepublicdiscourse.com/2011/07/3532/
[35] Ibid.

There are so many sad reasons for the rise in single parent homes, mostly the lack of sexual morality and basic godly life education. However, there is another rapidly growing reason. Many twenty-first century women in the world, now liberated from the chains of the past, feel they do not need men at all. They even go so far as to use sperm banks rather than have men involved in their lives. Some have swung the pendulum so far in the other direction that they have become female supremacists, belittling men and viewing them as secondary to women. Two wrongs never make a right.

If you are a woman, please hear me. If we walk in offense, or bitterness, or hostility, or even female supremacy, we are once again off the road of truth. Unfortunately, some of the pro-female Christian writing did just that; it would have a tinge of hostility or unforgiveness. Not of all it of course, but those other writings left me empty because the authors took me from one ditch, all the way across the road of truth, and into another ditch. Having accurate information without the right heart does not release love's power to affect change. Let me assure you, the enemy does not care what ditch you are stuck in. He does not care if you are a male supremacist or a female supremacist. He does not even care if you know the truth and yet are bitter, because he knows you will still end up in a powerless ditch.

As dark as things seem to be, there is still hope in God's original plan. No matter what the statistics may tell us, God is still at work. He is moving upon the hearts of men and women across the globe to rise up and face this giant. Strategically, there has not been another time such as this in human history when bigotry and discrimination were so widely believed to be inherently wrong.

The hearts of men and women are now ready for the revelation of this message. Even though some of it is contrary to what many have been taught in the Church, the Truth will ring true in their hearts. The Lord is making His Bride ready for a revolution of thinking that will bring forth a revival of spiritual life. My husband, Gregory, likes to call it a "renaissance"—a fresh, new move of God that fundamentally changes everything. He does not see a revival coming in small waves as it has in church history. Rather, he sees a major revival, with a surge of new life that brings forth creativity and the establishment of the Kingdom of Heaven on earth that we have never seen before.

The road that leads to this renaissance is the application of truth in love.

Six

Changing Glasses

Offense in the Kingdom is like kryptonite to Superman, but honor is like spinach to Popeye. Can you see that? Bitterness and unforgiveness drain the believer and disconnect us from our Source of power. Whereas honor taps into the very heart of God, sees the person or situation from Heaven's perspective, and infuses us with His grace and strength. Honor brings power. Honor is like the electricity inside a conduit. Let me show you two contrasting examples of how we can release the power to flow in and through us to transform our world.

First, take Nazareth as an example. Jesus could do no great miracles in his hometown because of the people's offense—their lack of honor—and their unbelief. These people watched Jesus grow up. They knew Him only by the flesh, so they did not honor him as a prophet, much less as the Son of God. Their attitude was basically, "We know him; this is just Mary's son. We know his brothers and sisters. Who does he think he is?"[36]

So they were offended at Him. But Jesus said to them, "A prophet is not without honor except in his own country, among his own relatives, and in his own house." Now He could do no mighty work there, except that He laid His hands on a

[36] Mark 6:1-3a

77

> ...honor is like spinach to Popeye.

few sick people and healed them. And He marveled because of their unbelief.

Mark 6:3b-6a, NKJV

Even Jesus Himself could not release the power of the Kingdom among these folks because of the presence of offense and the absence of honor. Without honor, there is no faith. Honor actually proves the existence of faith. You see, if they had believed, they would have honored Him, but this they did not do. Kingdom power is love, which is both released and received through the heart. Their attitude of offense hardened their heart toward Him, so He was unable to do many miracles there. It is incredible to think that their lack of honor and unbelief could actually stymie the Son of the Living God! Yet that is exactly what happened.

Can you see how offense in the Kingdom is like kryptonite to Superman? Conversely, honor is like spinach to Popeye. The faith released by honor can take a weakling and turn them into a powerhouse. As an example, let us take the Canaanite woman whose daughter was possessed by a demon to demonstrate how that works.

In Matthew chapter 15, we find the story of this Canaanite mother. She was not a Jew, so she was not part of the Abrahamic covenant. She was a Gentile and lived apart from the promises of God. Her demon-possessed daughter desperately needed a miracle. She knew who Jesus was and she believed, so she pursued Him for help. This Gentile woman shouted and cried out to get His attention. At first, He did not even respond. When the disciples complained about the ruckus she was causing, Jesus informed them that "He was only called to the lost sheep of Israel."[37] Meaning, she was not one of God's chosen. She was in a powerless position, outside the covenantal promises of God.

> Yet she received her miracle because she overcame the hurdle of offense.

That did not stop this mother who loved her daughter. She knew Jesus had the ability to help her. When she got the opportunity, she bowed before Him, making her request. Even though He had seemed to ignore her, she did not get offended, and she honored him! Jesus still told her, "No," and even went so far as to refer to her as a dog! "*And He answered and said, it is not good to take the children's bread and throw it to the dogs.*"[38] Healing was the children's bread, and she was not a child of Abraham. Yet she received her miracle because she overcame the hurdle of offense.

If I had just been called a dog, I think I would have been highly offended. My response would have been, "How dare you call me that?" Can you just see Jesus sitting there, probably smiling as He says something like, "C'mon lady, you're getting it!"? He was giving her an opportunity to get onto that powerful

---

[37]Matthew 15:24
[38]Matthew 15:26

Kingdom road. He was giving her a receptacle to plug into the power source. She did honor Him; she leapt the hurdle of offense and responded well:

> *But she said, "Yes, Lord; but even the dogs feed on the crumbs which fall from their masters' table." Then Jesus said to her, "O woman, your faith is great; it shall be done for you as you wish." And her daughter was healed at once.*
>
> Matthew 15:27-28

Can you see how she cleared the hurdle of offense and continued to walk in honor? She acknowledged Jesus as the Master of the table. Her honor and her unwillingness to take offense brought her onto that Kingdom road where she too could benefit from the children's bread. My translation of Jesus' response goes like this: "Girl, glad you ate your spinach 'cause you got it! You got your miracle!"

As we discover more about the Kingdom, walking in the miraculous will be normal. For us to follow Christ's example, we must be careful not to leave the road of truth and end up in a ditch. Offense toward anyone is a bump in the road that can easily divert us.

However, honor does not mean we ignore error or accept false teaching to be polite, politically correct, or to be accepted. Truth matters, and further,

> As we discover more about the Kingdom, walking in the miraculous will be normal.

it must always be truth in love to be "Kingdom." We must believe and apply the truth, for it is the truth that sets us free.[39]

Freedom is the fruit of truth! Lies always bind, so the enemy does not care which lie we believe as long as we do not believe truth. One of the easiest ways to recognize whether or not something is true is to examine the fruit. Does it produce freedom? If not, we should question from which kingdom it originates.

Now that we have properly set the stage, we are ready to examine 1 Corinthians 14:34-35 with a completely new filter. I encourage you to take off the old glasses and put on a new pair. "Lord, I pray You give each of us eyes to see exactly what You want us to see!"

To make certain we are viewing this controversial verse in context, let us put it in perspective with the previous chapters. 1 Corinthians chapter 12 is all about unity. The discussion centers on how every person can participate in the assembly. Paul clearly communicates that anyone can share a song or a word. The emphasis is on everybody being able to participate. The text goes on to explain that the meeting should be conducted in an orderly fashion so that it would not be chaotic with that many people involved. The text describes how no more than two or three should speak up front at one time. The whole point through this chapter is that everybody has something to bring to the gathering—*everybody*!

Next, the famous "Love Chapter" (1 Corinthians

---

[39] John 8:32

> It is hypocritical to open a door for a woman and say "ladies first," but then ask them to take a back seat or secondary role in areas of true importance.

13) is sandwiched in the middle of the discussion. It is a short but powerful description of how we should treat one another. It shows us how to walk in love—love is patient, it is kind, it is not proud, etc. This chapter is driving home the point that it is not all about you. Even if you are super-spiritual or highly-talented, if you are not walking in love you are nothing but a loud clanging cymbal, a worthless bunch of noise. Love does not draw attention to itself for it does not seek its own. Rather, love always defers one to another. Love always lifts others up and puts others first.

These rules of conduct have no gender distinctions. It does not say you should lift men up and put them first, but keep women down and put them last. It is hypocritical to open a door for a woman and say "ladies first," but then ask them to take a back seat or secondary role in areas of true importance. I appreciate it when my husband opens the door for me; it is a gesture of honor. However, even if he opened the door every time we stepped out of the house, I would not feel honored if he also refused to listen to my opinion on important matters. Those simple gestures become valuable only in context. Someone who bows nobly before a king, but then dishonors him behind his back is a hypocrite. For women who have had to struggle to overcome the gender barrier, the opening of a door can feel patronizing because they are perfectly capable of opening that door themselves. However, when the Queen of England pulls up in a limousine, you will never see her protest when the vehicle door is opened for her. She knows it is not about her capability; it is about her honor. Since my husband walks in honor toward me in every aspect of life, I do not feel belittled when he reaches for the door knob, rather I feel valued and respected.

Remember, the chapter divisions in our translations of the Bible were not in Paul's original letters. Chapters 12-14 are actually all part of one continuous discussion. If we are not careful, we can miss the vital connection of love and honor that flows through the Apostles instructions. In chapter 14, Paul continues to instruct the Corinthians concerning spiritual gifts. He is outlining how everybody has the opportunity to operate in these supernatural abilities. He starts by encouraging us to earnestly desire and pursue these gifts, especially that all would prophesy. He goes on to discuss how everyone can pray in tongues through their spirit, even though their mind may not understand. Similar to chapter 12, his point is that everybody can participate in this powerful, Holy Spirit filled stuff! These expressions of the spiritual gifts are not just for leaders; they are for *everybody*!

With everyone prophesying and praying in tongues all at the same time, it could certainly get confusing or chaotic. Paul once again gives the church

> …it is as if Paul turns on a dime.

at Corinth some healthy guidelines, which were never meant to restrict but to facilitate opportunity in an orderly manner.

Then all of a sudden, in verses 34-35, it is as if Paul turns on a dime. He does a complete 180 degree turn. Can you hear a loud screeching sound? Like an 18 wheeler going a hundred miles an hour, then slamming on the brakes while trying to turn completely around? For some reason, Paul suddenly shifts from chapter after chapter of unity and harmony, with full participation available for everyone in an organized fashion, to a completely contradictory statement:

Women are to keep silent in the churches; for they are not permitted to speak, but are to subject themselves, just as the law also says. If they desire to learn anything, let them ask their own husbands at home, for it is improper for a woman to speak in church.

1 Corinthians 14:34-35

The Greek word for "improper" here actually means "shameful" or "disgraceful."[40] So literally, verse 34 says it is *disgraceful* for a woman to speak in church. Wow! Can you imagine that? Really?

It actually says a woman should make no sound. None! This means no singing in the choir, no giving announcements, no teaching in the nursery.... I have

---

[40] Strong's #G149

84

never seen a church like that. In fact, in my experience, there are always more women participating in church than men, and naturally they all talk. Are we violating

> No one in Christendom honestly believes that women should not speak in church.

this scripture by letting them use their vocal chords?

These words seem clear, "women are to keep silent in the churches." I have yet to see ONE church anywhere, not even the most traditional, forbid women to make sound. Why is this? It is not because these churches find it impractical to enforce; we would all do it if we believed that was God's will. No one in Christendom honestly believes that women should not speak in church. Something is obviously wrong.

Our interpretation of this verse is problematic, and it gets worse. Paul adds that women should "subject themselves, just as the law also says." This should be another red flag that something is amiss. Such a command cannot be found in the Law anywhere. There is no such commandment in the Pentateuch[41] or even in the whole of the Old Testament. We do see plenty of cases where fallen man mistreated women, but you never see God issuing a commandment or edict which forces women to be subject to men. However, in most cultures, there was plenty of that kind of

---

[41] The Pentateuch is the first five books of the Bible, also called "The Law". The only verse that even comes close is in Genesis 3:16 ("He shall rule over you"). This is part of the curse; it is not God's original design. This is the fallen and twisted condition of mankind that Jesus came to restore.

anti-female sentiment. By Jesus' day it had become codified like law. During the time He walked the earth, women were even forbidden to learn the scriptures.

With the advent of Christianity, females were now being welcomed into the assembly where the Word was taught and discussed. Paul used women in ministry in almost every church he planted. Yet here in verse 35, it implies women really should not even learn in church.

If they desire to learn anything…

IF!? IF!?

If they desire to learn anything, let them ask their own husbands at home, for it is improper for a woman to speak in church.[42]

The literal interpretation of this verse indicates that women should not even ask a question in church. **Do not even ask a question!** Females should only be quiet, but they really have no place in learning. Do you really think that is God's heart? No way! That is not only completely contrary to the law of love, but it is also completely contradictory to the context in which it is written. Something else must be going on here; the question is "what?"

Have you ever seen the movie *National Treasure*? In the movie, there was a special pair of glasses that would reveal a secret treasure map, which was

---

[42] 1 Corinthians 14:35

hidden in plain sight. You could be staring right at the paper but not see it without those glasses on. The answer to this secret is also hidden in plain sight, but you will have to remove the lenses through which you have always looked so you can see the truth with a new set of eyes. We have removed our faulty filters, and we are now changing glasses. What you are getting to see will surprise you.

Seven

To Tell a Lie... Make it Big!

If anyone comes to Me, and does not hate his own father and mother and wife and children and brothers and sisters, yes, and even his own life, he cannot be My disciple.

Luke 14:26

At first glance, that verse in Luke seems to encourage the hatred of immediate family members. Some strange cults notwithstanding, do you know of any church that has a "hate your family rule?" Does the Bible teach the necessity of disliking or separating from parents, siblings, children, or spouse in order to be part of the Church? Of course not! But why not? Because we know that hating family members is not God's heart. We know His character and His love for the family. We also know many other scriptures that contradict such a preposterous notion. For example, we are exhorted to provide for our family, especially those in our own household.[43]

All Jesus is saying in that verse in Luke is that you should not let your family, or anyone else for that matter, be idols to you. Do not put them ahead of God in your life because the enemy could use them to trip you up. Your love and devotion to Him must be first and above all else. We never hear of a house of God requiring members to hate their own families. Maybe some crazy cult would, but no healthy

---

[43] 1 Timothy 5:8

Christian church would promote such a thing. Why not? Because we know that is not God's heart!

Our problem is that the enemy has been able to influence and affect our filters of interpretation. Ever since the fall, he has been twisting our thinking. Tragically, the enemy has sold us a pack of lies regarding the female gender. Because we believe these lies to be truth, we read a verse like "women are to keep silent in the church" and actually entertain it as if that could be the will of God. It is absolutely not! Silencing women is no more God's heart than hating your family!

Andy Andrews' book, *How Do You Kill 11 Million People?—Why the Truth Matters More than You Think*,[44] is a small little book—a very quick read, but it will haunt you with its implications. The book is about the Holocaust, and Andy makes a very powerful argument that Hitler was able to institutionally kill eleven million people (six million Jews and five million other Europeans) simply because they believed a lie. That is all it took to manipulate millions. Most of the victims of this insidious plot willingly got on those trains and unknowingly headed for the gas chambers.

Thousands of them would wait in the train yards and then pack themselves into the cars by the hundreds because they felt safe doing so. They would look around and only see maybe one armed guard way across the other side of the train yard. If they were

---

[44] Andrews, Andy, *How Do You Kill 11 Million People?—Why the Truth Matters More than You Think*. (Thomas Nelson, Nashville, TN) 2011.

not being forced to board the train car by the barrel of machine gun, then they figured there must be some truth to the propaganda that they were going to a better place. It was calculated manipulation by Hitler's regime. It was a planned lie, and these victims bought it by the hundreds of thousands. The multitudes could have easily overpowered the few armed men, but instead they got on those trains voluntarily. They believed they were being removed for their own good; that it was dangerous where they were, so they were being sent to somewhere safer. These poor people would look around frightened but not see a bunch of armed soldiers. So, they would think, "What the government is telling us must be true."

> ...if you tell a lie, and you make it big enough, and you repeat it often enough, people will begin to believe it.

The answer to the bone-chilling question "How Do You Kill 11 Million People?" is LIE TO THEM. **The devil knows if you tell a lie, and you make it big enough and you repeat it often enough, people will begin to believe it. Eventually the truth will not look true anymore.**

"How fortunate for leaders," Hitler said to his inner circle, "that men do not think. Make the lie big, make it simple, keep saying it, and eventually they will believe it."[45] In Hitler's autobiography, *Mein Kampf*, he wrote, "The great masses of the people will more

---

[45] Ibid, page 32.

easily fall victim to a big lie than a small one."[46] What is so crazy about that statement is that this book was widely read by the German people at the time. They should have realized he was lying to them! Many believed him anyway. Others simply did nothing—they ignored him. The passive are as guilty as those who drove the trains.

Similarly, we have been under the influence of the second greatest lie ever sold to the human race. The first lie took place in the Garden when we fell prey to the notion that we could not trust God's word or His intentions toward us. Everyone has struggled with that falsehood. The second greatest lie is that it is God's will for women to be separate from and unequal to men. The hierarchical view of men over women has been so woven into the fabric of history, that it seems natural. The fact that this is a lie seems almost too huge to be fathomable.

It is a lie, and this book is exposing it for what it is. God is removing the old veil that has blinded us. We are removing the old filter that makes something seem true, when in reality it is false. We are putting on new glasses so we can see the truth right in front of us. **All it took for women to become secondary was for us to believe that women were supposed to be secondary!** All it took for us to yield to the lie was for us to believe that it was true. That is exactly what has happened. We bought the lie, and we got on the train.

For a Christian, all it takes for us to keep that old

---

[46] Ibid, page 32.

Chaldee lie going is: 1) to refuse to believe the truth and pretend that the lie is actually God's will—that it is His heart; or 2) be passive and to refuse to confront the lie, even when we see the evidence and its devastation all around us. I pray neither you nor I will fall into either of those categories.

Put on your new glasses. You are going to see something hidden in plain sight. I want you to take a close look at what Paul immediately said after the "be silent and don't ask questions" statements in verses 34 and 35. Look at what comes next in verse 36:

Was it from you that the word of God first went forth? Or has it come to you only?[47]

Although many translations do not catch it, this verse actually begins with a disjunctive participle in the Greek. It is a tiny little "e" with a line over it: *ē*.[48] Author and theologian Gilbert Bilezikian says this:

"Recent scholarship has called attention to the disjunctive force of the participle *ē* that introduces verse 36. It has the impact of an emphatic repudiation of what precedes it. A colloquial equivalent such as 'Nonsense!' would come close to rendering the break between the prohibition statement (vv. 33-35) and Paul's response to it in verse 36."[49]

---

[47] 1 Corinthians 14:36
[48] Strong's #G2228
[49] Gilbert Bilezikian, *Beyond Sex Roles: What the Bible Says About a Woman's Place in Church and Family* (Grand Rapids, MI: Baker Academic, 3rd Edition – 2006) p. 115.

> He is refuting the anti-female sentiments so popular in his day!

That tiny little participle, which is often overlooked, has the effect of a strong repudiation of what was previously stated. Verse 36 should start with a negative exclamation. The *Revised Standard Version* presents the impact of Paul's response in verse 36:

> **What! Did the word of God originate with you, or are you the only one it has reached?**[50]

Can you see that Paul just contradicted, even blasted, what was said in the previous two verses?! **He is refuting those anti-female sentiments so popular in his day!** Are you able to picture it? If not, take a moment to shake off that faulty filter.

In chapters 12-14, Paul is being all-inclusive, encouraging everyone to participate. Suddenly in Chapter 14, verses 34-35, Paul makes a radical shift. Either he is having a schizophrenic moment, is being sarcastic, or he is directly confronting that false belief. I do not think the Apostle was schizophrenic. He may have been being sarcastic or using hyperbole, but more likely he was quoting the contentious Corinthians to directly rebuff that false position. He was refuting the prevailing doctrine of his day. This is the only way to interpret verse 36, and put the discussion back in context with the previous chapters.

---

[50] 1 Corinthians 14:36, RSV

The notions that women should not be able to learn or to speak in public did not originate from God's Law. They came from the wrong kingdom. What is Paul's response to these horrific statements and chauvinistic traditions? He says, *"What! Was it from you that the Word of God first went forth, or has it come for you only?"*[51] Meaning women can speak forth the Word of God, and they can receive and learn from it, because it was given to them as well.

PAUL WAS SILENCING THOSE WHO WANTED TO SILENCE THE WOMEN!

Can you see it now? Is your filter still foggy? Is it clearing up? Those verses will never look the same again once the light of truth shines on them!

Later in the series, we will also take a long look at 1 Corinthians 11, where Paul discusses hair length, head coverings, and the like. Paul was definitely dealing with a bunch of very contentious church members in Corinth who struggled with immorality on one hand and performance based Christianity on the other. They wanted to place legalistic restrictions on a free people. In the beginning of Chapter 7, Paul says, "Now concerning the things about which you wrote…." Paul was directly responding to a letter that they had written to him. It could very well be that Paul was quoting from that Corinthian letter when he penned the "women are to be silent" verse. That makes sense in the light of verse 36, where he completely renounces that notion. We cannot know for certain if he was quoting the false teachers, but there is no

---

[51] 1 Corinthians 14:36, NASB

doubt that throughout his epistle, Paul is dealing with their questions, statements, problems, and traditions.

The bottom line is this: Paul was not limiting the women, and he was definitely NOT telling them to be silent!

You cannot take that verse and somehow magically claim, "Well, Paul really did not mean total silence, rather he meant to restrict and limit women." I have actually heard otherwise brilliant men make that very claim. They say that Paul did not mean what he actually said; he did not mean total silence. Rather, they assert that what he meant was that the women are to be submissive to the men in the church, and therefore they are not to teach adult men nor to hold positions of authority. Sadly, even today, this verse is used to prevent women from being pastors, teachers, and elders.[52] (We will look further at the subject of elders in Book Eight of this series, *Nobility's Rule*.) Either God is a God of honor and inclusion, as Paul so beautifully demonstrates in the rest of chapters 12-14, or women are to be restricted from leadership with their voices muzzled. You cannot have it both ways.

Thankfully, there are many female–friendly churches today. However, most of these choose not to deal directly with the prohibitory verses (like 1 Corinthians 14:34-35) because they are obviously very, very anti-female. They do not want to get involved in a controversy for which they have no biblical answer as to why they allow women to teach or lead. Most of

---

[52] Timothy 2:12

these churches have the right heart, but they have not discovered the revelatory truth you are receiving in

> …women are freer, but chains still do exist.

this book. In these institutions, women are freer, but chains still do exist.

Without these new glasses to see the truth, some folks try to explain away the prohibitions by saying they were only culturally relevant to Paul's day—meaning women had to be silent back then, but they do not have to now. In their proposition, women in the Corinth church were immature. They were being loud and disruptive, shouting out questions to their husbands from across the assembly. I do not know where that interpretation started, but it does not fit with the context of the chapter nor does it make any sense given the strict, prohibitive culture of that day. Women would not have gone from total silence to unruly, loud public behavior. Moreover, Paul did not say here, "speak quietly." That verse literally forbade even a sound come from a woman in church.

Some of our more charismatic, prophetic type churches want very much to empower women. Most still struggle with where to draw the line. They believe there must be a boundary for women somewhere because of these prohibitory scriptures. Therefore, to empower women and yet honor the Word, they will set the bar as high as they feel comfortable. There is a huge difference in where that bar is set, depending upon the church or denomination you visit. In most

> To fully reflect God's image in the boardroom, both masculine and feminine voices are necessary.

churches today, there are still some type of gender-based restrictions because of the false belief that the scriptures indicate one is necessary.

Some churches allow women to hold every office in the church except that of elder.[53] Others may allow female elders, but they purposely choose women who think like them—they choose women who most closely reflect the male leadership currently in power. They fear that females in general would not be able to handle conflict with the men. They also fear that adding women to the leadership structure would bring too much change too quickly. So female elder selections are based on how well she can fit into the current male dominated structure. This practice defeats the very purpose of having women join the leadership team in the first place. To fully reflect God's image in the boardroom, both masculine and feminine voices are necessary. One is not better than the other—even if it is different than yours.

In other churches, the line is drawn way up near the very top. Meaning a woman could be a pastor or elder, but she could not hold the senior-most leadership position. If she were married to the senior leader, then she can be a co-leader for her husband would still be above her. However, she cannot hold

---

[53] 1 Timothy 3:1-13

the top position on a hierarchical basis, for that role is reserved for a male. This practice is justified by quoting these exact verses in 1 Corinthians 14 (along with those in chapter 11, and 1 Timothy 2) as the basis for limiting a woman in senior leadership.

That is an exegetical nightmare. You cannot possibly use the verse in 1 Corinthians 14, which totally silences women, as the basis for allowing them to hold positions of leadership but with some restrictions. It would take some kind of hermeneutical gymnastics to take the verses that say "be silent, do not ask questions" and make them mean she can be an associate pastor but not the senior leader.

Neither can you ignore this verse which says "no sound" and still allow women to sing in choir and teach kids, but at the same time use it in your argument to restrict them from teaching adult men. You do not need a Doctorate in Divinity to know you cannot interpret scripture that way. If you are of this persuasion, please remove that verse from your argument.

There is a wide diversity on the application of gender restrictions in the Bride of Christ today. Many of our fundamental and evangelical style churches hold to the traditional view of fully restricting women from authority. On the other hand, many of our charismatic churches have very limited restrictions for females. Some of these restrictions may not even be noticeable unless you were looking for them. These churches retain just enough *Chaldee* to draw a gender line somewhere in their structure. Sadly, this

> She could be President of the United States but not senior leader of a church?

too will cause them to slide off the powerful Kingdom road of truth and into a ditch.

The traditional position seems absurd to those in the world outside the church, where women can be CEO's of billion dollar corporations or prime ministers of nations. They look at the church as archaic. They do not understand why a woman could be trusted with a Fortune 500 corporation but not a 50-person congregation. She could be President of the United States but not senior leader of a church?

Such thinking would seem ridiculous unless you believe the female gender restrictions were indeed God's will expressed through Paul's words. It would make sense that church leadership would have an obligation to discriminate against women, if the traditional interpretation of these verses was indeed God's divine order. Most church leaders today know that discrimination and lack of freedom is contrary to God's love, so they are confused and torn between Paul's words and God's heart. Thankfully, *Crown Her a King* is going to reconcile the discrepancies and free these leaders to follow God's heart and His Word!

I pray you are now seeing that any limitations placed on women based on 1 Corinthians 14:34-35 are not God's will. That doctrine is a train car built by the enemy. It is a lie intentionally planted by the enemy to subvert and disempower the Church. Paul never meant to silence or limit women. In fact, his purpose in those very verses was to do the exact opposite! He was silencing those who wanted to keep women in their subservient place.

The cancerous *Chaldee* lie was designed to harm God's people, not to protect them. It was calculated manipulation on satan's part. Like the lies of Hitler that orchestrated the Holocaust, this is "an intricate web of lies… designed to ensure the cooperation of the condemned (but unknowingly)."[54]

The cooperation of the condemned has been canceled. We no longer buy the lie!

[54] Andrews, *How Do You Kill 11 Million People?*, page 23.

Eight

From Cursed to Crowned

If you are a man, many of the books in this series will strengthen you as a godly leader. They will empower and encourage you to be all that God created you to be. You will discover how to take dominion over yourself and over the enemy. I pray before you reach the end of the series, you will know beyond a shadow of a doubt that you are royalty—a king and a priest in God's Kingdom on the earth. On behalf of all women, I sincerely apologize for the burdens that have been unfairly heaped on you. You were never meant to carry the entire load alone. Please forgive us for buying the lies of the enemy and not staying by your side!

If you are a woman, you are going to be amazed at the level of freedom to which you are called. God was never limiting you—not ever! It is my prayer that this book has begun dismantling any chains holding you back because of your gender. I pray by the end of this series that you will find complete freedom in Christ and in the Church. Remember as you travel on this road toward liberty, do not allow yourself to get bitter or resentful toward those who believed the lies. You cannot go from one ditch to the other. You cannot now get mad, or bitter, or resentful at the people who taught you the lies. They believed those restrictions were true.

Most men in the church who hold to the more traditional view only do so because they honestly think they are honoring the scriptures. There are a few evil

> Forgiveness is the toll to the road of freedom.

people in the world, but for the most part those who hold to the more restrictive interpretation of a woman's position in church are good people who simply believed the lie! I believed it too when I first started this walk. We have all been deceived at one time or another. If you need to get mad at anyone, get mad at the devil; he is the father of lies.[55]

For our struggle is not against flesh and blood, but against the rulers, against the powers, against the world forces of this darkness, against the spiritual forces of wickedness in the heavenly places.[56]

We must now understand how important it is to walk in forgiveness. **Forgiveness is the toll to the road of freedom.** We must also walk in honor and humility. We are going to learn throughout this series, particularly in Book Six, *Your Royal Identity*, who we truly are as nobility—as royalty. We are all a whole lot more powerful and glorious than we ever dreamed possible.

The glory which You have given Me I have given to them, that they may be one, just as We are one; I in them and You in Me, that they

[55] John 8:44
[56] Ephesians 6:12

*may be perfected in unity, so that the world
may know that You sent Me, and loved them,
even as You have loved Me.*

John 17:22-23

Our power will come from our unity—unity
with the Lord and unity with each other. Honor is
the mortar that joins us together. Therefore, we must
walk in honor, but we must also walk in truth. One
is hollow without the other. We will dive deeper into
the concept of biblical unity in Book Nine, *United We
Stand*....

There is another lie we need quickly to debunk
before we close this book. Were you ever taught that
the order of creation proves that the men have a divine right, and therefore responsibility, to rule over
the women? This teaching declares that since the man
was created first and the woman was created second,
therefore the man rules. I was actually taught that in
church as if it was fact, but it does not follow the biblical pattern. Look at the order of creation. First, God
created the inanimate objects like dirt, rocks, sun,
moon, stars, etc. Next, He made simple life forms that
occupy the bottom of the food chain such as plants
and trees. Then He creates the birds of the air and the
fish of the sea. He begins day six by creating the animals, and then He finishes up by creating mankind,
male and female. Notice the progression? How does
the order of creation prove that men have a divine
right and responsibility to rule over women? It does
not!

We will also look at headship later in the series, which is a very important Kingdom concept. I can assure you, however, that Kingdom headship has nothing to do with "ruling over" anybody. God's created design did not establish any organizational structure where men ruled over women! We are not supposed to be ruling over each other—period. The woman being created last does not mean she has a divine right to rule over the man. In God's Kingdom, man and woman are to rule together, side by side, over the earth. We are to take dominion and rule like God, as ONE. We are to rule over the fish of the sea, the birds of the air, every creeping thing—even over the enemy who will be crushed under our feet.[57] We are not supposed to be lording over other human beings. That is the pattern of the *wrong* kingdom!

When satan entered the Garden, he sold us lies that led to the fall. Part of the curse on the woman was that "your desire will be for your husband, and he will rule over you."[58]   The word for "desire" here is the same word used to describe what sin wanted to do to Cain in Genesis chapter 4. Cain was upset because God approved his brother Able's sacrifice but not his. Cain's countenance fell; he was despondent. The Lord warned him not to open the door for sin to come in and control him. God told Cain:

> *If you do well, will not your countenance be lifted up? And if you do not do well, sin is*

---

[57] Romans 16:19
[58] Genesis 3:16

*crouching at the door; and its **desire is for you**, but you must **master** it.*

Genesis 4:7

Sin's "desire is for you" meant that sin wanted to master and control Cain. As a re-sult of the curse from the fall, no longer would the first couple be united, side by side ruling over the earth. Now they would turn on each another. Her desire would be to control her husband, but he would rule over her. Please understand that was not God's design for the Garden! That is not His heart, and that is not His will! It is a result of the curse. The division between man and woman is not God's plan. **It is the curse!** It originates from the wrong kingdom!

> As a result of the curse from the fall, no longer would the first couple be united, side by side, ruling over the earth.

Who was given dominion over the earth? We were. God gave it to mankind. Whatever kingdom we come into agreement with, that is the kingdom empowered to influence the earth. When we agree with the enemy, evil prevails. Look around. Watch the news. The sad proof of this is everywhere.

Even though mankind fell, we still have domin-ion. We can empower lies or we can empower the truth. Guess what is established when we come into agreement with God's will? His Kingdom! Yes, that was exactly the Lord's prayer:

Our Father who is in heaven,
Hallowed be Your name.
Your kingdom come.
Your will be done,
On earth as it is in heaven.

Matthew 6:9-10

We have the power to turn this world around! The problems may seem insurmountable, but nothing is bigger than our God. He is obviously not forcing His will on us. Look at sex trafficking or abortion statistics. Are those wicked things the will of God? Of course not!

We did not lose our dominion in the fall. Psalm 8 takes place after the fall but before the cross, and man still has dominion just like in the Garden. We will discuss this concept deeper in Book Seven, *Taking Dominion*, but for now, please understand that you have way more influence and power over your world than the enemy wants you to believe. We can empower the kingdom of darkness by believing lies, or we can empower the Kingdom of Light by embracing His truth.

Also remember that when satan came after the female in the Garden, he was not just coming after man's bride; he was ultimately out to destroy Christ's Bride! It is Christ's Church who will take off satan's head. Partnering with our Groom, we will decapitate and disempower

> We did not lose our dominion in the fall.

108

him once and for all.

Satan has been after the female from the very beginning. The scripture says that the enmity would be between the devil and the woman, then also be

> The enemy is going to be sorry he ever messed with the woman!

between his seed and her Seed. Seed in many translations is capitalized because it refers to Christ, who will deliver the fatal blow to his head. Notice that the enmity was not just between satan and her Seed, it was first between satan and the woman. "And I will put enmity between you and the woman, and between your seed and her seed…."[59]

The enemy has been against women since the fall! He has been at war against us. We accepted the assaults of the limitations put on us. We did so because we thought this was the way things were supposed to be. He managed to get our cooperation in his scheme! But it was another one of his lies! Now, we are taking back ground! Together, men and women are reclaiming our rightful position on this earth! We are reclaiming our dominion. **The enemy is going to be sorry he ever messed with the woman!**

As Kris Vallotton so aptly points out, the curse against satan is that the woman would be at enmity with him! His curse was not just to crawl on his belly and eat dust. The enemy's curse was that women would turn on him. His punishment was that he would receive the women's wrath, and ultimately

---

[59] Genesis 3:15a

> *Crown Her a King is about Restoring God's Glory to the Bride of Christ.*

the wrath of the Bride of Christ! Now that we know the truth, it is payback time! Not against flesh and blood—not against human men—but against the devil, that serpent of old. It is time for us to take off his head!

The next step in our strategy must be to become better acquainted with this Kingdom Jesus wants to establish on earth. Our job is to usurp the serpent's reign on the earth. Book Two, *The Gospel of Kingdom,* will help us to do just that. As we come to understand and manifest this magnificent Kingdom of Heaven, we will realize how and why the Church got the women issue so wrong. The *Crown Her a King* series will deal with this controversial subject head on, but the teaching is much broader than just the women issue. All of us, men and women alike, will be empowered to take dominion. We will learn to reign as kings and to worship as priests. We will learn what it means to be noble and to love with radical abandon. We will even discover that there has been a *Great Mystery* sealed up for this very hour.

Regardless of our gender, we are all sons of God. We are all the Bride of Christ. We are all kings in His Kingdom.

Crown Her a King is about *Restoring God's Glory to the Bride of Christ.* It is about breaking off the chains of the enemy from the bride of man so that

God's glory can be restored to the Bride of Christ. It is about breaking chains off His Church as a whole so she can arise from her current condition of being weak, divided, and powerless. When we as individuals rise up and take on our royal identity and unite together, we will be an unstoppable force. His beautiful, beloved Bride will become all that God intended her to be! She will become a Bride worthy of her Groom!

These are great days we live in. We are transitioning from being poisoned with cancerous *Chaldee* to being positioned as kings. We will unite as a community, drive out the enemy from our land, and install the rightful King of kings on the throne. We will restore the world to its original design—I do not mean fig leaves and gardening. I mean a world where an intimate relationship with God and with others is possible. Where love and honor replace fear and selfishness. Where the power and grace of the Holy Spirit is manifest all around us. Where poverty is replaced by abundance, and where the influence of the evil one becomes nothing but a distant memory. If you think this is pure fantasy, nothing more than a fairy tale, then I pray the Lord reawaken your ability to dream and your sense of adventure. *"All things are possible to him who believes."*[60] The battle is indeed real, but so is the possibility of victory!

We are to complete the assignment Christ left for His Body to accomplish: We are to establish God's Kingdom on the earth. It is time for the Bride to arise from her sick bed and take her rightful place of

---

[60] Mark 9:23

authority and influence. She shall become ONE with her Groom. Together Christ and His Church will take dominion and subdue the earth. The enemy is going to be sorry he ever messed with the Bride because we are moving from cursed to crowned! *Crown HER a King!*

Group Discussion Questions

1) How would you describe the problem, "Cancerous *Chaldee*"?

   Is it hard to imagine that you could possibly have on a faulty filter?

   Or, does knowing this bring new clarity to old issues?

2) In what specific ways have the traditions and doctrines of men influenced your experience in the church? In the business world?

   In what ways were these positive?

   In what ways were these negative?

3) If you are female, name a few ways in which you were treated differently because of your gender. If you are male, name a few ways in which you have treated women differently than men.

   In what ways were these positive?

   In what ways were these negative?

4) Jesus said in John 8:32, "You will know the truth, and the truth will make you free."

   How does this verse apply to the *Chaldee* problem?

   Does it bring you hope? Why or why not?

Going Deeper
Private Time Questions

1) Understanding why we think a certain way is important. We are influenced by those around us, particularly as we are growing up. Ask the Lord to show you what important people in your life thought about women and their role in the world. Also ask Him to show you how that influenced or affected you. Use a notebook or separate sheets of paper to journal what God shows you.

   a. For example, what was your mother's view of women in marriage? In the home? In the church, leadership or otherwise? In the business world?

   b. Also ask, "Lord, is there anything else about my mother's opinions on women that I need to know?"

   c. Repeat "a" and "b" above for your father, church, society in general, and your spouse or someone else particularly close to you.

   d. Looking back over your answers to the above, try to fill in the grid on the next pages with just one or two words to summarize what the Lord showed you.

   e. If you did not grow up with your mom or dad, then please substitute another male and female who were influential in your formative years.

2) As the Lord leads, please intentionally and specifically forgive those who negatively influenced you toward the female gender—whether they did it from false beliefs or because they acted in an ungodly manner, or whether they were male supremacists or female supremacists, manipulating women or controlling men—whatever...

If someone in your past negatively affected your opinion of the female gender, you need to acknowledge it and then forgive them. Forgive them whether they understood that they were wrong or not.

I recommend specifically journaling out your prayers of forgiveness for each person.

Do not skip this forgiveness step!!!!

Offense is always a tool of the enemy, even if you are not aware that you are carrying it!

	Mother's	Father's	Church's	Society's	Spouse/Closest
Marriage					
Home					
Church					
Business					
Other					

About the Series

Crown Her a King™
Restoring God's Glory to the Bride of Christ

Crown Her a King is a series of 12 small, power-packed books that take a unique look at the core subjects required to have victory in our battle to establish God's Kingdom on earth. This series covers such topics as the believer's royal identity, hearing God's voice, taking dominion, the great mystery, and more. Woven throughout the series is the women issue, as it a key to restoring God's glory to the Bride of Christ. The series lays out a revelatory strategy for ushering in a renaissance in the church, a lasting revival that brings spiritual life to the world. Each book in the series is a stand-alone message, and all are an integral part of the whole. Audio messages, taught from a live classroom, that contain the core of each book are available from www.KingdomBrewing.com.

Book One:
Cancerous Chaldee

The world is fallen, selfish, divided and weak. And sadly, the church is not much better off. One primary reason for this is the divisiveness between people, particularly men and women. The Apostle Paul preached grace and freedom from bondage to the law; he did not subvert women, although many traditionally believe that he did. Jesus said the traditions and doctrines of men render the Word of

God as void of power. The anti-female traditions we now deal with have become a cancer which infected and weakened the Church. Thankfully there is a cure for this disease which has robbed His Beloved of her splendor. This journey will restore God's truth to the Church and reveal her true identity in the Kingdom as Christ's glorious, noble, united, and powerful Bride.

Book Two:
The Gospel of the Kingdom

Jesus came preaching the Gospel of the Kingdom, not just the gospel of salvation. While healing, He would say, "the Kingdom has come upon you." He was constantly demonstrating Heaven's will being done on earth. It was a reality to be experienced in the here and now. But this Kingdom's power source is love, not control. Love does not seek its own, and love by definition always offers you a choice. If it is it forced then it is not love. God never forces His will on any of us. This is a very different Kingdom from the world we live in where the people want power so their own will can be done. But this is not the world as God designed it. His original plan for mankind was twofold: intimacy and dominion. We were to be one with Him, one with each other. And we were to subdue the earth—not each other. God's original mandate has not changed.

Book Three:
Who's the Helper?

Unity was the key to our power, so satan's main objective was to get us to divide. Since we have dominion here, he has to gain influence over the earth through people. He attacked the crowning jewel of creation and has been at war against her ever since. Divided we remain powerless, living behind self-protecting walls of shame or blame. There has been a huge misunderstanding in interpreting the verses in creation regarding the "helper" or "help meet." But that word should never have been applied to a human being. If man's bride believes she is supposed to be an assistant in life rather than a full partner in war, she shrinks back and ultimately violates the purpose of their relationship. Man is once again alone as the two live with walls between them. There is no power in co-existing. It takes both male and female united AS ONE to reflect God's image and glory on the earth.

Book Four:
Lies that Bind

How did satan get us to divide? How did he get us to doubt God? With a lie that appeared to be true. When a lie appears true, truth appears false. Why is truth so important? You are more powerful than your enemy so he cannot bind you unless he gets you to believe and agree with him. Lies put you in bondage; truth sets you free. Truth is like a powerful but narrow road with a ditch on either side. The enemy does not care what ditch you are in so long as he keeps you off the center of that powerful, liberating path. On one side is the supremacist ditch which claims it is God's will for women to be secondary; on the other side is extreme feminism which bitterly reacts to abuses from the past. To carefully maneuver the Church out of the supremacist ditch, we need to comprehend how this lie took root and why the Church is still stuck. As we pull Her from the miry mud, God's truth will prevail and freedom will indeed reign.

Book Five:
The Groom's Voice

Before truth can be accepted, it must be based on God's VOICE. "Did God really say?" We have to know for ourselves what God said in His Word as well as what He is currently saying. Jesus withstood the enemy by quoting scripture that declared, "Man shall not live on bread alone, but on every word that PROCEEDS out of the mouth of God." Even Immanuel could do nothing on His own initiative, but only that which He saw the Father do or heard the Father say. To be in unity with Him and with each other, the voice of God must be as real to us as it was to them in the Garden. Based on the teachings of Mark Virkler, we will explore four easy steps to learn how to hear and honor God's Voice. The creator of the universe lives inside us and is closer than our skin. To be one with Him we must recognize and voluntarily yield to His loving voice. Through wounded hearts the enemy gets us to listen to the wrong voices, so inner healing becomes a key to being a powerful yet safe person.

Recognizing His voice is the key to victory in every arena of life.

Book Six:
Your Royal Identity

We are a royal priesthood, joint heirs with Christ, a Kingdom of kings. We are children of the King, and He gave us a divine mandate to rule the earth. But there has been a major problem: both the fallen and the redeemed alike live out of their woundedness rather than out of their royal identity. Based on the teachings of Kris Vallotton, we will explore the difference between how princes and paupers think and behave. Paupers focus on their lack, kings imagine possibilities. Our internal reality always determines our outcome. Just like Joseph and Daniel, if we are royalty on the inside then it does not matter what circumstances we fall into. Even as slaves, these men rose to the top and ruled nations. Because they were powerful on the inside, their external circumstances yielded to their internal reality. We are the head and not the tail. Only as kings can we fulfill our royal mandate to destroy the works of the enemy and establish God's Kingdom on earth.

Book Seven:
Taking Dominion

We must take dominion! We must take dominion over the enemy and over the earth. The legal right to rule is already ours, but we've been allowing the forces of evil to prevail. We did not lose our dominion at the fall, rather what we lost was our identity. All of mankind has dominion—whether saved or unsaved. Therefore, all it takes for evil to prevail is for people to give into temptation. We are either empowering the kingdom of darkness or the Kingdom of light. Before we can rule over evil forces, we must first be able to rule our own flesh. We cannot possess authority over any spirits that we make agreement with—like addiction or depression. Additionally, in order to wield authority on the earth, we must first be submitted to authority. Debunking lies about women's role in leadership will restore the scepter to the Church's right hand.

Book Eight:
Nobility's Rule

Unity is the key to power, and honor is the key to unity. Only if we walk in honor can we walk together. God's Kingdom is an upside down kingdom where the least is greatest, where you give to gain, where you die to live. As nobility, as kings in this upside down kingdom, we rule through love. Because we know we are powerful, we never serve from a slave's mentality. We know how to go the extra mile, because it is a "get-to" not a "have-to." We do not submit from a place of slavery but rather from a place of strength. We can put others before ourselves because we do not operate out of insecurity or lack. Honor and faith are substances that connect us to God's Kingdom in the here and now, where miracles become normal. This is an inclusive Kingdom; there is room for all to be saved, and there is room for all to be kings. And no one has to cover their head, or walk in someone else's shadow, or live with their faces or their glory veiled. Instead, we lift each other up and by doing so we all go higher.

Book Nine:
United We Stand...

Our differences are meant to be the very places of our joining together, like puzzle pieces. Take a husband and wife for example; it is in the very place of our physical differences that God designed us to experience oneness physically. Boy has the enemy perverted that one! Man and wife were to be a plural unity, in God's image. United we stand; divided we fall. Divided we are alone. And a kingdom divided against itself cannot stand. Jesus said in John 17, the answer to world evangelism is that we become one, like They are One. We are to connect with each another at varying levels of intimacy, so there needs to be healthy and natural boundaries. When these boundaries get twisted, we get confused and again our dominion suffers. Never before has the family unit become so broken that normal bonding in infancy and childhood is absent or distorted. When we are joined together properly, living stones neatly fitted together, we are one unstoppable force. The Church is a sleeping giant—ready to wake up!

Book Ten:
True Worship, True Love

Originally this message was going to be *Undaunted*, a message about the history of women. Since the fall of mankind women have had it rough. For modern women, the level of freedom we now enjoy came at a huge cost to many before us. Our freedom was not free. Many undaunted men and women have fought and paid a huge price for the liberties we now take for granted.

God changed our plans. Instead of *Undaunted*, He took us on a journey into *True Worship, True Love*. He took us through the elements of the tabernacle where we find Christ and the plan of His redemptive work. From the beginning of time God wanted to dwell with us and bring His Kingdom to earth—first in the Garden, then in the tabernacle, now inside our very beings. We are the temple; we are God's dwelling place. Having a deep and abiding understanding of true worship comes from understanding God's work on the earth despite our fallenness. The tabernacle was the perfect means for demonstrating *True Worship, True Love*. It was also the perfect example of covenant and that there was a mystery yet to be solved.

Book Eleven:
The Great Mystery

In every epic story ever written, there is a battle between good and evil, usually involving both a hero and a damsel in distress. This theme is woven into the very core of our being and has been since the beginning because such a battle literally rages in the spirit realm. The damsel in distress, however, is not just any female, she is the Bride of Christ. Yes, the truth is that man's bride has been taken captive by the enemy. But as Paul says, "this mystery is great but I speak of Christ and the Church." The issue is much larger than gender. It is about the whole Church. Covenant is a living reality. If a married couple is united as one but half of her glory is veiled, then both are held back. If as the Bride of Christ we are to be connected with each and one with Him, but half the Church has her glory veiled, then we are all held back. Our Groom is awaiting a glorious Bride. It is time for the unveiling. Only together, corporately AS ONE, can we truly take our dominion of the earth, disciple nations, and replace the dark overlord with the King of kings and establish His glorious Kingdom on earth.

Book Twelve:
Her Coronation

God created the male and the female for the purpose of intimacy and dominion. All creation has been groaning for the manifestation of the sons of God—for us to wake up to who we really are and to establish God's Kingdom on earth. Now that the lies have been exposed and replaced with truth, male and female will once again rule side by side, together. We are all royalty, made in God's image. Now that we comprehend our royal identity, we will be undaunted because we fight from victory not for victory. No longer do we strive to gain power by ruling over each other, instead our strength comes from unity, love, and from the very presence of the Holy Spirit. Together, in partnership with the Lord and each other, we will change the world. We will establish God's Kingdom on earth. The Bride will be fully baptized in glory, in the Holy Spirit, and in good works. Christ will return for a Bride worthy of her Groom. But first, as the Church, we must crown her a king.

About the Author

Susan Dewbrew is a gifted and passionate teacher. She has an amazing tenacity for seeking truth and dispensing it with love and clarity. As much of an intellectual as she is a nurturer, she has a keen ability to instruct and encourage every believer in the fulfillment  of their own personal calling and destiny.

Susan honestly believes that God not only wants the Church to change the world for the better, but also that He is empowering all believers to do just that. She has a vision to see individual lives so transformed that the kingdoms of this world become the Kingdom of our Lord. Like Joan of Arc of old, Susan wants to see God's Army rally together and unite the nation to drive out the enemy and install the rightful King on the throne. You will often hear her say, "together we can do it!!"

Prior to opening her "tent-making" business in real estate, Susan was on staff at Convergence Church in Fort Worth, Texas as a Ministry Strategist where she also founded and led their Healing Rooms ministry. She is serious about seeing people healed physically, emotionally, spiritually, intellectually, relationally, and financially.

Susan is never far away from a good cup of coffee and never too busy to encourage someone in the Lord. She values her Bible education even above her Bachelor of Arts degree obtained from the prestigious and historic Washington College in Chestertown, Maryland.

She is madly in love with her husband Gregory who has devoted his life to feeding the poor. Together they have four amazing children and three grandchildren who have Gramma and Pops right where they want them!

You can connect with the Dewbrews via email at

info@KingdomBrewing.com

or

info@CrownHerAKing.com